The Anglo Concertina Music of
Phil Ham

Gary Coover

ROLLSTON PRESS

ISBN-13: 978-1-953208-08-8

All titles are in the public domain unless otherwise noted.

Front cover and title page photos by Jen Ham

Interior photos provided by Phil Ham

Also from Rollston Press: The Anglo Concertina Music of John Watcham (2020)
The Anglo Concertina Music of John Kirkpatrick (2021)

ROLLSTON PRESS
1717 Ala Wai Blvd #1703
Honolulu, HI 96815
USA
info@rollstonpress.com

PREFACE

While working with John Kirkpatrick and John Watcham on books about their Anglo concertina playing, both mentioned Phil Ham as being an early inspiration who had greatly influenced their styles of playing.

I was not previously familiar with Phil other than hearing a couple of his recordings on an old cassette tape issued by the Morris Ring back in the 1970's. There have been no other commercial recordings and he never played in any bands that made recordings, so his purported influence was a great mystery.

Both John K and John W had lost touch with Phil over the years, with no idea as to his whereabouts or if he was even still around. It was only through some very diligent and fortuitous research that I was finally able to locate Phil in northern England near Newcastle-upon-Tyne. And the good news is that he is indeed quite alive and doing well and still playing the Anglo concertina at the grand age of 92 years old!

It has been an utter delight to meet up and work with Phil on this project – he has such a wealth of information and memories of a lifetime of playing music, and he readily supplied the many historical photographs for this book as well as a detailed biography of his life with the Anglo concertina.

Back in 1982 he made a cassette tape of Morris tunes for the Newcastle Morris Men that had "a small but enthusiastic circulation" and in 1984 he recorded a private cassette of tunes from the Ascot-under-Wychwood tradition. There are also recordings of his playing from 1976 that are on the International Concertina Association website. In 2019 he made a tape of some local tunes and sea shanties. With Phil's blessing, many of the tunes from these various tapes are linked to the transcriptions via scannable QR codes.

Most of Phil's playing has been for English traditional Morris teams, so many of those tunes are included here. But his musical interests extend way beyond the Morris so some of these are included as well, all with the same easy-to-use tablature system used in all the other Rollston Press concertina books.

It is indeed an honor and a pleasure to be able to transcribe and present to you the historical and influential Anglo concertina playing of Phil Ham.

Gary Coover

Editor/Publisher
Rollston Press

N.B. If you would like to learn Phil's wonderful arrangement of the Bledington Morris tune "Ladies of Pleasure", see *The Anglo Concertina Music of John Watcham*, Rollston Press, 2020.

FOREWORD

There are certain moments in your life that you can pinpoint, even after many years, as events that will shape the future. One of mine is hearing the Anglo concertina when I was 14, standing outside The Doves in Hammersmith.

Inspired by Peter Boyce, who had formed the Chingford County High Lads' Morris team, I had just taken up playing an English concertina for the side. In true Morris tradition, Peter had arranged for us to join a pub-crawl - and it was outside that riverside pub that I first knew what an Anglo sounded like and fell in love. It was being played with such consummate skill for the dance and I could scarcely believe that such a small instrument could produce a sound so musical and lyrical. It was, of course, being played by Phil Ham, and I instantly knew that the Anglo was the one for me. I think that Peter, too, knew that this was the way forward and he arranged for me to visit Phil at home to hear more of his playing. Not only was this inspirational, but Phil most kindly lent me a 26 key Jones instrument. What a flying start! I was indeed hooked, not only by the instrument - time line, chords, rhythm just made for Morris - but also by Phil's style of playing.

Another such moment of great fortune in my life was meeting Gary Coover way back in the late 70's - and on and off, we've kept in touch ever since. Gary's passion for the concertina knows no bounds and I was more than flattered when he approached me with the idea of publishing a book of my playing, based on his vast recorded library of Anglo players. When writing the foreword to this book, I paid tribute to Phil's playing, but couldn't say much more, as I had lost touch with him for about fifty years. However, it was this passing remark that led Gary to track Phil down - not only alive and kicking at 92, but with a fine back catalogue of recordings. It has been my greatest pleasure to be reacquainted with tunes that set me on the road and also to hear many more that exemplify the delightful and skilful player that he is.

I hope that through Gary's lovingly meticulous work, you too may enjoy playing in Phil's style and be inspired to use his techniques to expand and improve your own playing. Enjoy!

John Watcham

July 2022

TABLE OF CONTENTS

Introduction 7

English Morris Dancing 8

The Anglo Concertina in 10 Minutes 9

A Short Introduction to the Harmonic Style of Playing 11

Keyboard & Tablature 13

Tunes 15

A Great and Mighty Wonder 17

A-Roving 18

Bacca Pipes 19

Bacca Pipes 20

Balance the Straw 21

Balancy Straw 22

Banbury Bill 23

The Banks of the Dee 24

Beaux of London City 26

Billy Boy 27

The Black Joke 28

Blaydon Races 29

Blow the Man Down 30

The Bluebells of Scotland 31

Bobbing Around 32

Bobby Shaftoe 33

Bound for the Rio Grande 34

Country Gardens 35

Dearest Dicky 36

Double Lead Through 38

The Dressed Ship 40

Drunken Sailor 41

Fine Knacks for Ladies 42

Fire Down Below 43

Getting Upstairs 44

The Geud Man of Ballangigh 45

Handkerchief Dance 46

Here's to the Maiden 48

Highland Mary 49

Hunt the Squirrel 50

I Saw Three Ships 51

Jockey to the Fair 52

Johnny Come Down to Hilo 54

The Keel Row 56

Lads-a Bunchum 58

Maid of the Mill 59

Maypole Dance 60

Milley's Bequest 63

Monk's March 64

Mrs Casey 66

Mrs Casey 67

None So Pretty 68

Now is the Month of Maying 70

The Nutting Girl 72

On Ilkley Moor Baht 'At 74

Princess Royal 75

The Quaker 76

Rodney 77

The Rose 78

Santy Anna 80

Shenandoah 81

Sheriff's Ride 82

Since First I Saw Your Face 83

Strike it Up, Tabor 84

Trumpet Tune in D 85

Trunkles 86

Twenty-Ninth of May 88

Valentine 89

Vandalls of Hammerwich 90

The Vicar of Bray 91

William & Nancy 92

Notes on the Tunes 95

My Journey with the Anglo Concertina 105

Introduction

"Phil Ham" is not a name that instantly comes to mind when talking about notable Anglo concertina players, yet his innovative playing style in the 1960's and 1970's influenced many of today's top players. John Kirkpatrick and John Watcham both credit Phil as an early mentor.

But Phil was much more than just an early influencer – he was a major innovator who was one of the first to play the Anglo concertina in a harmonic style by playing across the rows.

In the 1960's, Reverend Kenneth N.J. Loveless and Phil Ham were the two major Anglo concertina players playing Morris dance music in England. While Rev. Loveless mostly played in Kimber's choppy and mostly single-row style, Phil explored the many possibilities of intricate accompaniments that could be found anywhere on the instrument regardless of which row the notes were on.

Phil has spent most of his career playing for traditional English Morris dancers, and his style has a solid dance foundation that is often accented by the needs of the accompanying dance steps. He also plays hymns and madrigals, and several are included in this book.

Although he plays a Jeffries concertina with more than 30-buttons and with Jeffries accidentals on the right-hand top row, all of Phil's tunes here have been arranged here to be played on the more common 30-button C/G Anglo concertina with Wheatstone/Lachenal accidentals. A few of the tunes required very minor accommodations, but most are exactly as arranged and played by Phil.

The tunes are presented with the same easy-to-learn button number tablature found in all the Rollston Press concertina books, and every tune also has a Button Map showing exactly which buttons are needed to play that tune.

AND... every tune is accompanied by a QR code which links to a corresponding historical recording of Phil playing the tune. Most smartphones can automatically scan QR codes.

The recordings of Morris music typically have an initial A part that is played before the dancers start and is known as "Once to Yourself".

English Morris Dancing

One of the oldest forms of traditional folk dance still performed today, Morris Dancing is an English institution dating back many centuries, some say to the 1400's or even earlier. The dance's origins are lost in the mist of time. Are they vestiges of ancient pagan fertility rites? Or did they devolve from court masques and dances from the time of Henry VII? Even the origin of the word "Morris" is still a matter of some debate.

Known as "sides", many Morris Teams can trace their history back over several generations and even up to 200 years. There are several different styles of traditional Morris, with Cotswold Morris being the most common, but there is also Welsh Border Morris, East Anglian Molly dance, Northwest Clog Morris, and Rapper and Longsword dances that are part of the tradition.

The Cotswold tradition in Oxfordshire and Gloucestershire typically consists of dancers lined up in two rows of three dancers each, plus a musician and a fool, and sometimes other peripheral characters like a Hobby Horse or a Betsy (a man dressed as a woman). Characteristic features of the dancers' "kit" include white shirts and pants, handkerchiefs, wooden sticks, bells, baldrics, ribbons, flowers and hats.

Each dance has its own specific tune, often tied to a specific village or tradition, and the tunes come from a variety of sources, from late Medieval to adaptations of 18th and 19th century popular music. Most performances take place outdoors during the summer, at public houses, fetes, and festivals, and sometimes the dancers also perform traditional Mumming plays. Dancing out on Boxing Day and the First of May is still very much a Morris tradition.

By the end of the 19th century the custom had largely died out and would perhaps have been forgotten if it had not been for a chance encounter between folksong collector Cecil Sharp and the Headington Quarry Morris Men on Boxing Day in 1899. He subsequently recorded many of the tunes and dances played by their Anglo concertina player, William Kimber.

Sharp's interest in the tradition resulted in a revival of many of the dances, and with the later Folk Revival of the 1960's and 1970's there was an explosion of interest in Morris Dancing. Many new sides were subsequently founded in the UK and the US and there are now approximately 1,000 Morris teams worldwide. There are four Morris sides with an unbroken tradition still dancing today.

THE ANGLO CONCERTINA IN 10 MINUTES

originally published in *English Dance & Song*, April 1966
© *English Folk Dance & Song Society. Used with Permission.*

The Anglo Concertina in ten minutes by P. A. L. Ham

I MAINTAIN that only an idiot would attempt to write an article on how to play an instrument in ten minutes, but the Editor has been most persistent with me so I presume he must know what he's doing.

Maybe you've read the earlier articles in this Magazine*, in which case you'll know that a concertina player has four different fingering systems to choose from; the *Anglo* is the one in which each button produces a different note on push and pull of the bellows. It's the folkiest instrument of them all, and, I think, the easiest. Most of the concertinas you see around now are, in fact, the *English* type (The Enemy) and the number of Anglo players in the country can be numbered on the buttons of one keyboard. However, with rare exceptions (such as Bacup) the English concertina had its heyday in the Victorian drawing-room as a strictly classical violin replacement; the thing you found in rough pubs was more likely an Anglo.

Now down to brass tacks. First of all let us take a look at you. Your musical training is pretty negligible, but you have a sense of rhythm, a good ear for a tune and wouldn't mind being able to knock out a few folk songs or Morris dances by ear on the Anglo concertina? Fine. You're the type we're looking for.

The first thing you have to do with the instrument is pick it up. Some people get bogged at this stage and either give up or resort to hanging it round their necks with string or only playing it on their knee when sitting down or something. Feeble stuff. To get the correct hold, put the palm of each hand

* "English Dance and Song," March, 1963, and September, 1963.

(that is, the part with four fingers appended) through the straps so that the thumbs are left free. The right thumb should come neatly over the air-valve. If now you have the straps correctly adjusted—and this means to the nearest sixteenth of an inch or so—you will be able to arch the palms of your hands so that the ball of each thumb presses down on the frets and you have gripped the instrument while still leaving your fingers free to waggle.

So far, so good. Let's think of the air-valve next. The player of any push-pull (or blow-suck) instrument is a lucky man indeed if he finds a tune with equal rations of push and pull. You'll have to learn from the very start to work the air-valve continuously, as you play, in order to keep the bellows about half extended. Stopping in the middle to take a breath is cheating.

Now let's look at how the notes are arranged. As you may know, the Anglo concertina, unlike the English type, has treble notes on the right hand and bass notes on the left. On a 30-key instrument they are laid out in three rows of five on each side, so that the fingers fall naturally along the rows. If we take the inner row for each hand the complete set follows the push-pull pattern for a ten-key melodion, split into two. See Professor Rundle in the April, 1964, issue for details (one of the perks of delayed authorship). The next row is the same, only pitched a fifth lower, and is usually considered the main key of the instrument; hence it *is* normally found to be C. The outer row has enough chromatics for a full scale plus extra notes such as G on pull, which gives extra versatility.

Many people get all horrified at the thought of having to learn where all the notes are on an instrument. Use stealth. Confine yourself to the middle rows on each hand to start with and try pressing the buttons one at a time to see what comes out. There are only ten so it's not asking much. Do it while pushing the bellows in, then while pulling them out. Follow this up by pressing the buttons in pairs; then try threes, and so on. Try and use all your fingers on both hands at one time and another.

After a few evenings of these tuneless melodies (if you've still got a home) you'll be on nodding terms with the notes and might well graduate to simple tunes such as Bobby Shaftoe and the like. Now is the time to get hold of all those song books, or anything which can suggest titles for you to play. Try 'em all; any you can't cope with in the first five minutes leave alone for the while and press on to the next. If you come across a tune with an ' accidental ', which means an odd sharp or flat, just poke around and see if you can find it in one of the other rows. It is possible to play in minor or modal keys as well as the major ones provided; in effect you just start in a different place.

I hope you won't be content with playing just one note at a time on the Anglo concertina; the disadvantages of being stuck with a very few keys it's easy to play in are compensated for by the ease with which you can put in simple accompaniments in those keys. Besides, it doesn't half make a wonderful racket when you have the hang of it. There are various techniques; it is easy to play in thirds by pressing adjacent buttons, or in sixths by following a tune played on the right hand with a similar thing pitched lower on the left. Almost any combination of buttons in the appropriate row on the left hand will produce a passable vamp for a start.

In general, for morris dances, you want block chords, played pretty staccato in order not to drown the tune. In fact your whole finger and bellows-work wants to be alive and vigorous; the dancers haven't left the telly just to go to sleep listening to you, you know. Most tunes need no more than three chords, and about as much as I've got space for as the tenth minute looms up, is given below.

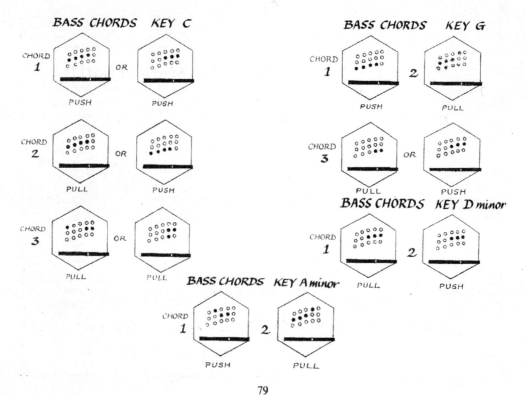

79

A Short Introduction to the Harmonic Style of Playing

Over many years of playing the Anglo Concertina, I did not have any idea what "The Harmonic Style" actually meant; it seemed to be a natural thing to play in Harmony based on my early musical background. For many people starting off to learn however, it could be helpful to put it all into context first.

Many much-respected musical instruments are only designed to play one note at a time. On the other hand, keyboard instruments and those with several strings would enable to play a tune and many other notes at the same time. It is thus possible to play a tune and an "accompaniment" in several kinds of ways, and in all sorts of styles. This is the "Harmonic Style" with "Chords" (combinations of notes) and other tricks which have been in the musical repertoire for centuries.

The Anglo Concertina basically provides two rows of buttons, each row having all the notes of a major scale (usually C and G) divided up between Push and Pull of the bellows. The higher notes are given to the Right hand and the lower notes to the Left – so you have got all you need to play a simple tune. But you *do* also have the ability to play other notes at the same time and make some sort of accompaniment.

As it happens, due to the way the notes are distributed it is easy to get a number of handy musical chords – on both Push and Pull – which you can call on for an accompaniment. The third row of buttons on a 30-button Anglo adds a number of sharps and flats, as well as a few buttons which give you repeated notes – the other way round: Pull/Push instead of Push/Pull. This is all veryuseful, because it enables you to play some sequences more smoothly *and* to add several new Chords to your repertoire.

There is plenty of music which you can play on an Anglo Concertina with no more than this range of facilities. You do need, however, to pay attention to how you use the Push/Pull combination in order to get the notes of the Tune *and* those of the Chords to coincide as required.

You also need to think about the 'management' of the bellows. Always begin with the bellows about half-extended, but if you don't get a more or less equal use of Push and Pull whilst playing, then you could end up with the bellows either shut or fully extended. If you find yourself heading for such a place then you need to work the air-valve at just the right time during a Push (or Pull) to get some air in (or out) as the case may be.

And, as far as possible, you should always play the accompaniment so that it doesn't drown the Tune. This means not grabbing a handful of buttons whenever you need a chord, but limiting yourself to three (or even two) notes – *and* perhaps making the chords just slightly shorter than the corresponding notes in the Tune.

Finally, you should remember that the bellows are not only a source of wind to make the reeds speak, they are also the means to play loudly or softly, and to add expression into your playing. The violinist has his bow, you have your bellows; think of them like that.

You will find examples of all these techniques in the various tunes you can listen to in this Book; I have included a few short notes here and there to point you in the right direction; also have a look at the 1965 Article for Chord patterns. Above all: the best way to learn is to really enjoy what you are doing!

Phil Ham.

KEYBOARD & TABLATURE

The button numbering system used here for 30-button Anglo concertinas in the key of C/G:

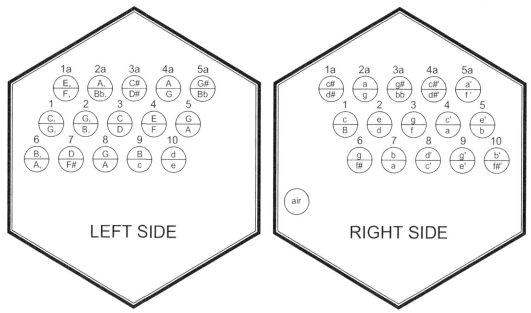

LEFT SIDE   RIGHT SIDE

Low notes are on the left side of the instrument and high notes are on the right. Notes shown above the line are on the push, notes shown below the line are on the pull. Standard abc notation has been used to show the pitches of the notes.

How the tablature works in this book:

- The buttons are numbered using the "1a-10" numbering system for each side.
- Buttons on the right-hand side are shown above the musical notes.
- Buttons on the left-hand side are shown below the musical notes.
- Notes on the push are shown by button number only.
- Notes on the pull are shown by button number with a line across the top.
- Long phrases all on the pull will have one long continuous line above the button numbers.
- Notes that are held longer indicated with dashed lines after the button number.

EXAMPLE:

Each tune also has a Button Map showing the buttons needed to play that particular tune:

Buttons played

TUNES

A Great and Mighty Wonder

(Es Ist Ein Ros)

Buttons played

Cologne Gesangbuch, 1599

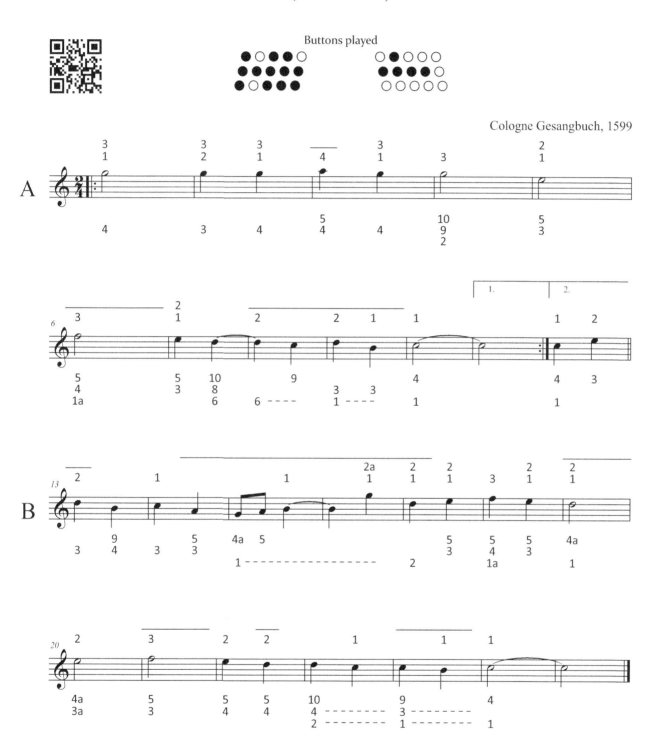

A-Roving

Buttons played

Traditional

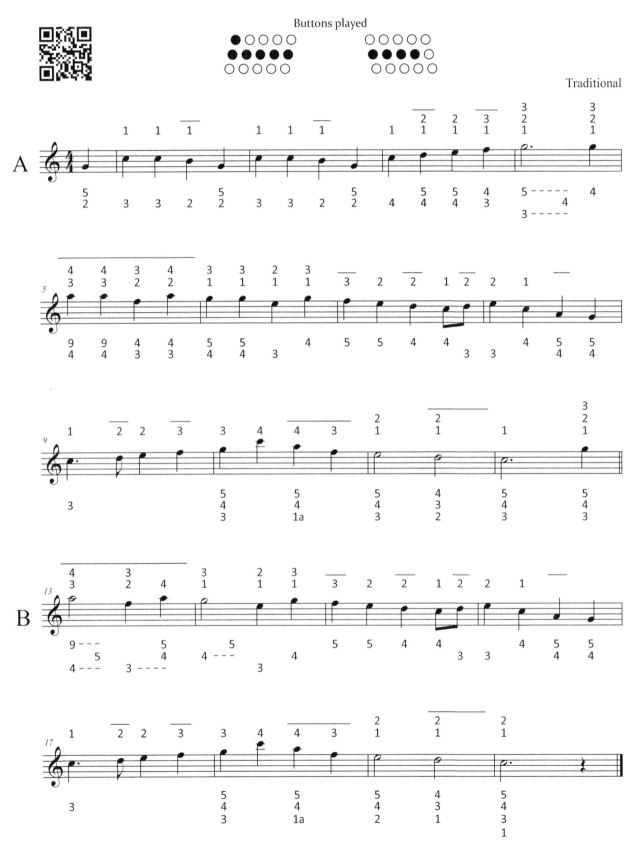

       The Anglo Concertina Music of Phil Ham

BACCA PIPES

(Ascot-under-Wychwood)

Buttons played

Traditional

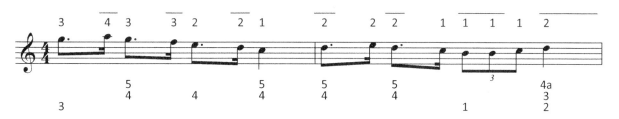

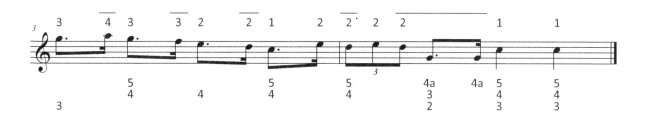

BACCA PIPES

(Headington)

Buttons played

Traditional

A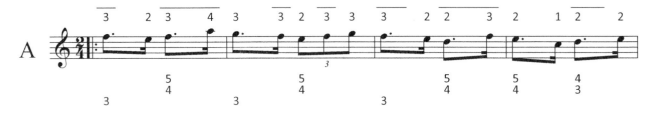

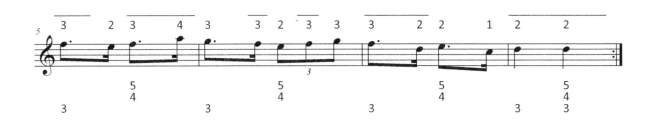

B

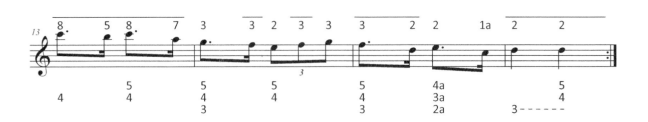

20

The Anglo Concertina Music of Phil Ham

Balance the Straw

(Field Town)

Buttons played

Traditional

Balancy Straw

(Ascot-under-Wychwood)

Buttons played

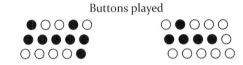

Traditional

The Anglo Concertina Music of Phil Ham

Banbury Bill

(Bampton)

Buttons played

Traditional

A

B
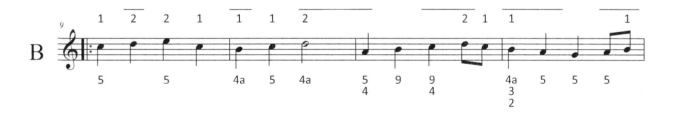

Banks of the Dee

(Field Town)

Buttons played

Traditional

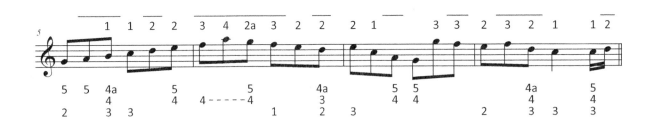

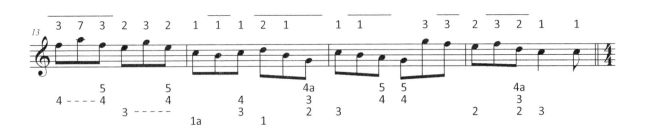

Beaux of London City

(Badby)

Buttons played

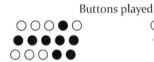

Traditional

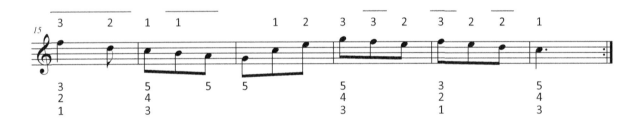

Billy Boy

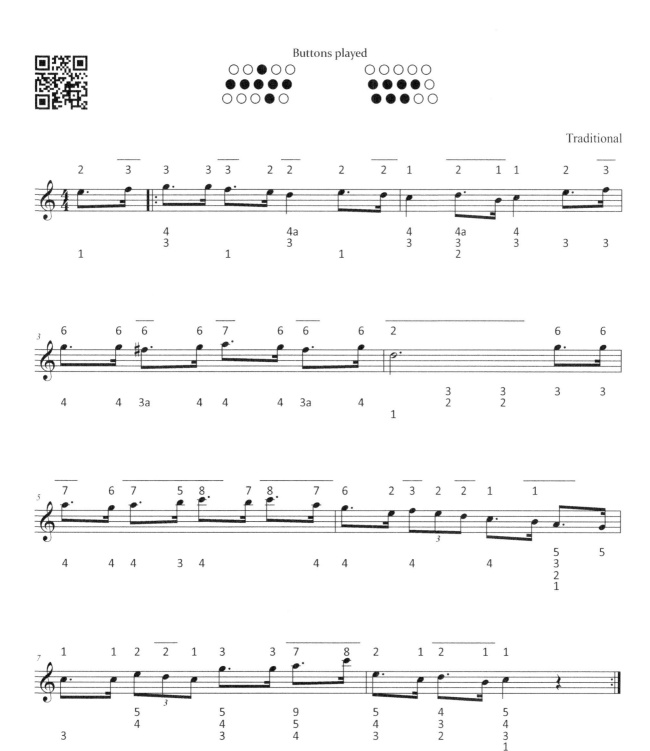

Buttons played

Traditional

The Black Joke

(Ilmington)

Blaydon Races

Buttons played

Traditional

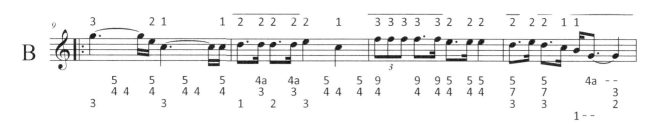

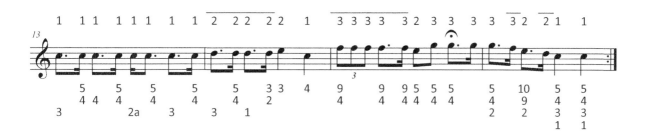

Blow the Man Down

Buttons played

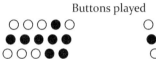

Traditional

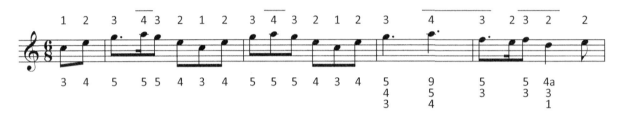

THE BLUEBELLS OF SCOTLAND

Buttons played

Traditional

Bobbing Around

(Bampton)

Buttons played

Traditional

A

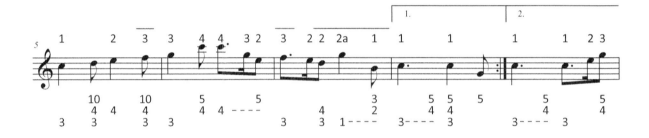

B

The Anglo Concertina Music of Phil Ham

Bobby Shaftoe

Buttons played

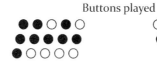

Traditional

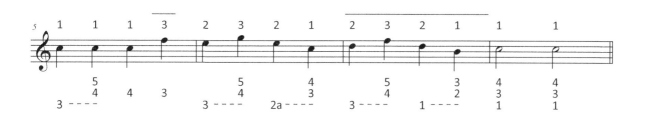

Bound for the Rio Grande

Buttons played

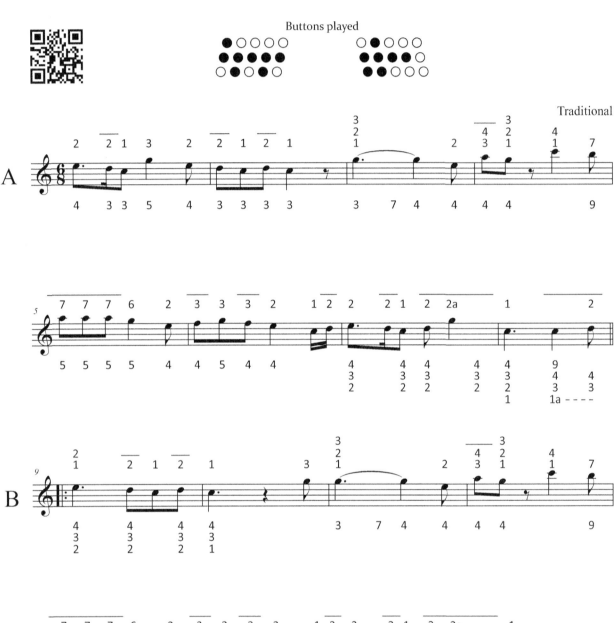

Traditional

COUNTRY GARDENS

(Field Town)

Buttons played

Traditional

Dearest Dicky

(Field Town)

Buttons played

Traditional

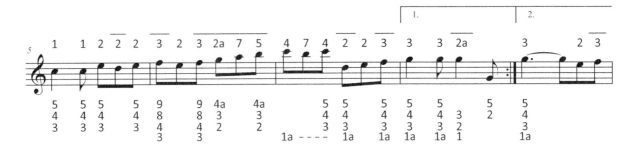

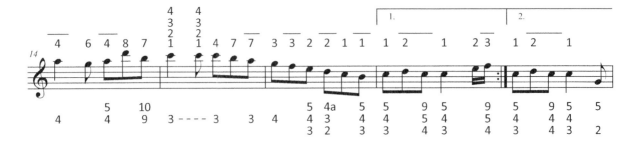

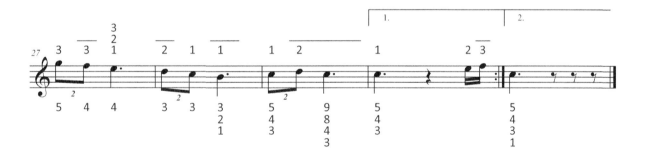

Double Lead Through

Buttons played

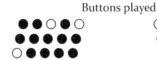

Traditional

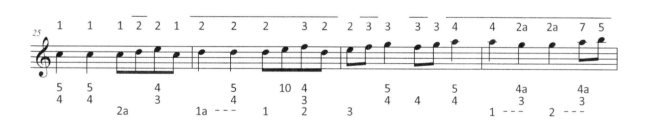

The Dressed Ship

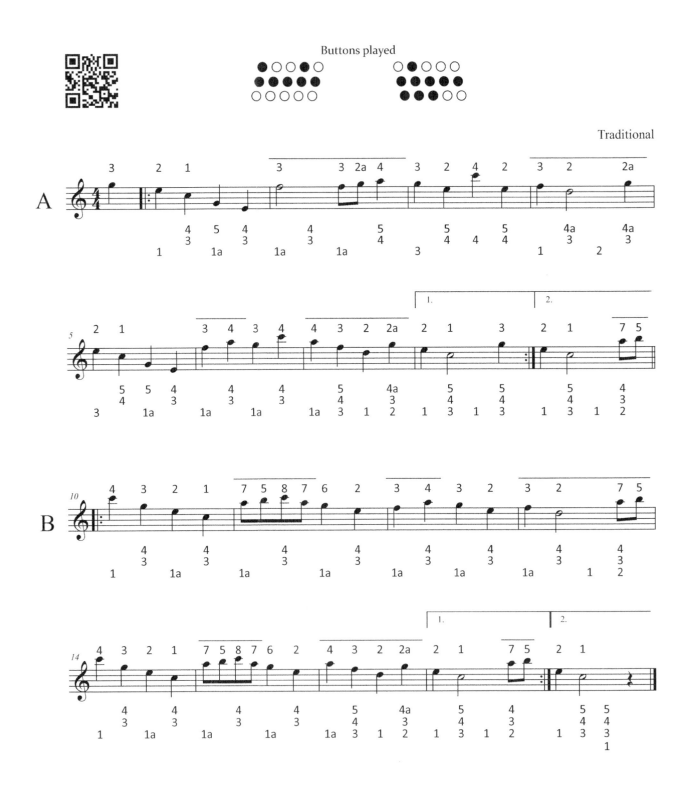

Traditional

Drunken Sailor

Buttons played

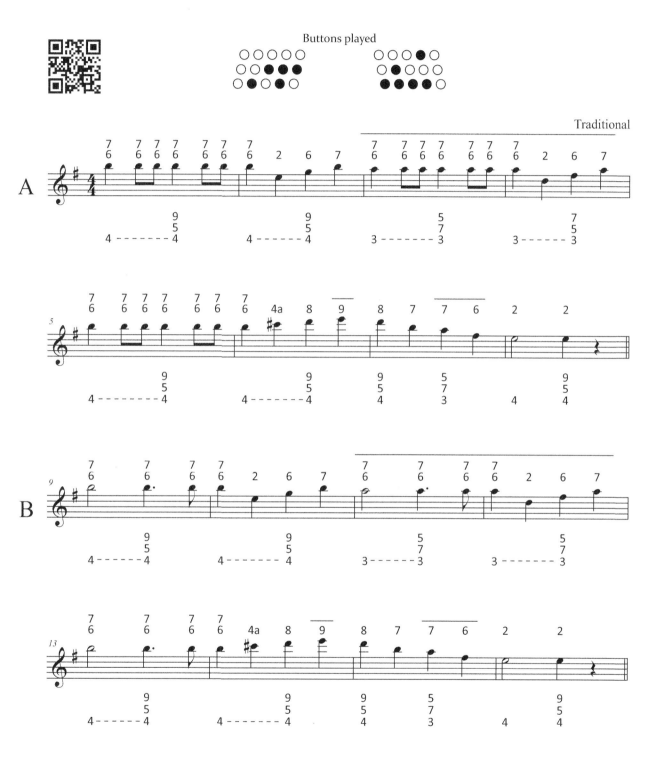

Traditional

Fine Knacks for Ladies

Buttons played

John Dowland (1600)

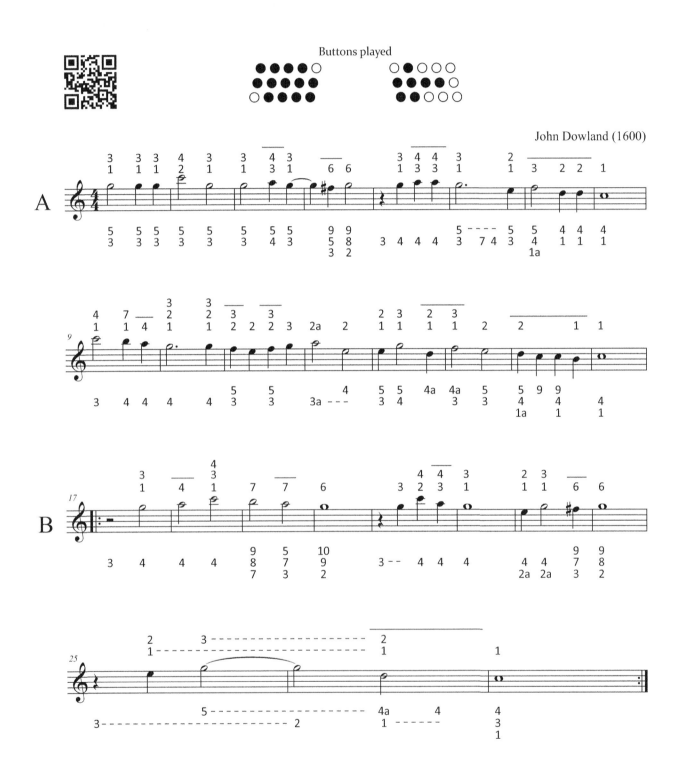

Fire Down Below

Traditional

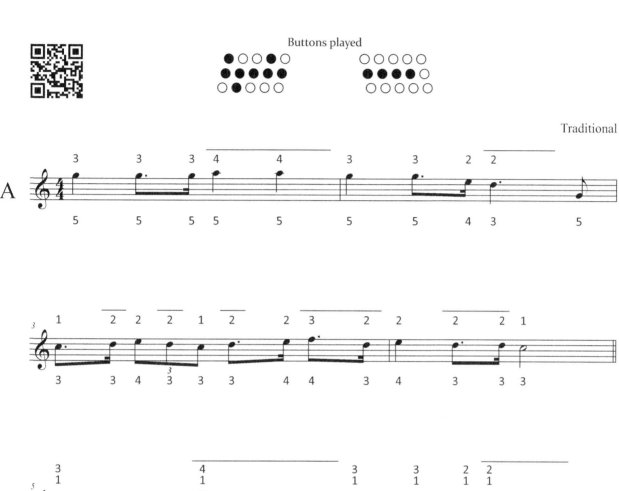

GETTING UPSTAIRS

(Headington)

Buttons played

Traditional

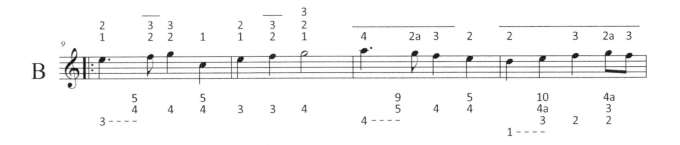

GEUD MAN OF BALLANGIGH

Buttons played

Traditional

A

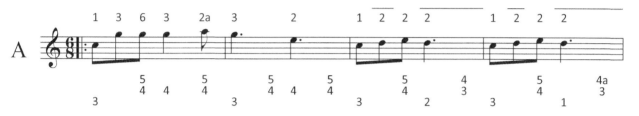

B

HANDKERCHIEF DANCE

(Upton-on-Severn)

Buttons played

Traditional

A

B

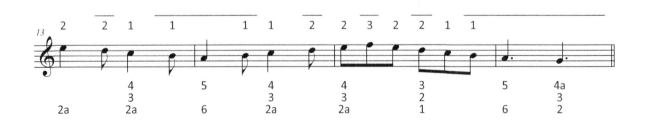

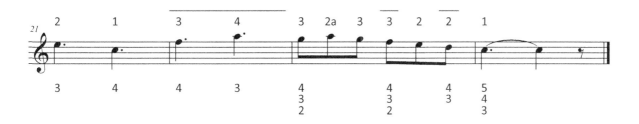

HERE'S TO THE MAIDEN

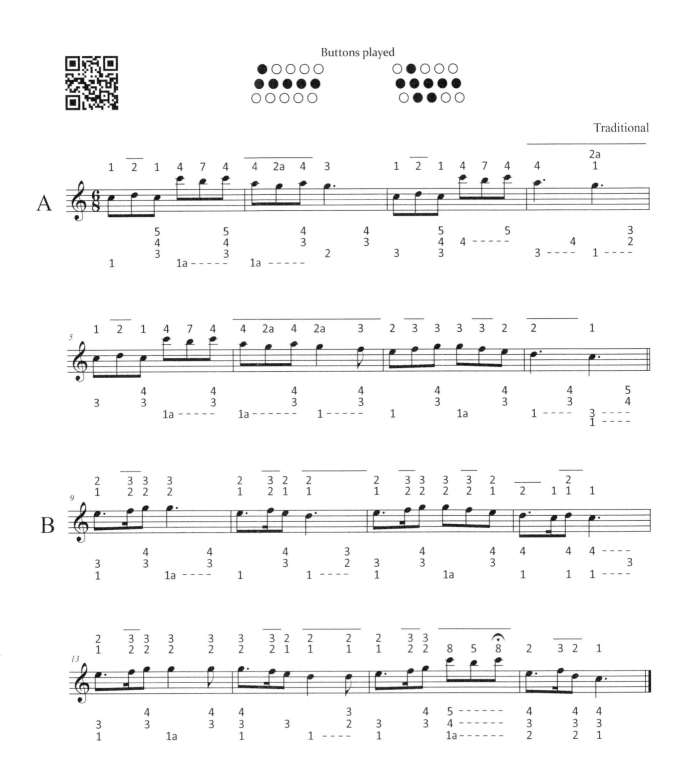

Highland Mary

(Ascot-under-Wychwood)

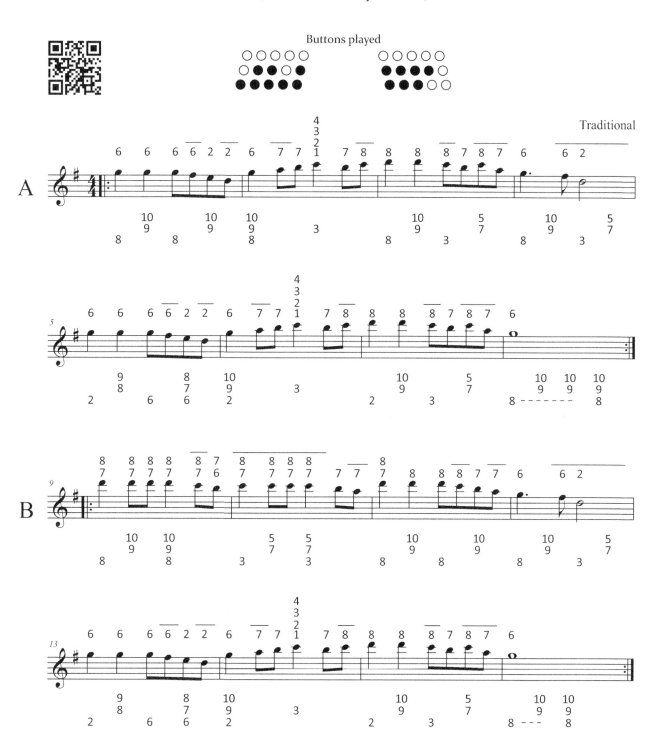

Hunt the Squirrel

(Headington)

Buttons played

Traditional

A

B

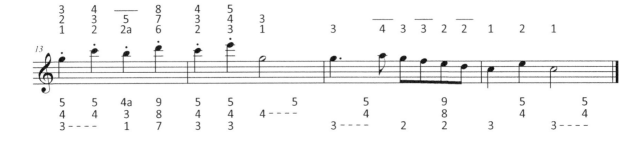

The Anglo Concertina Music of Phil Ham

I Saw Three Ships

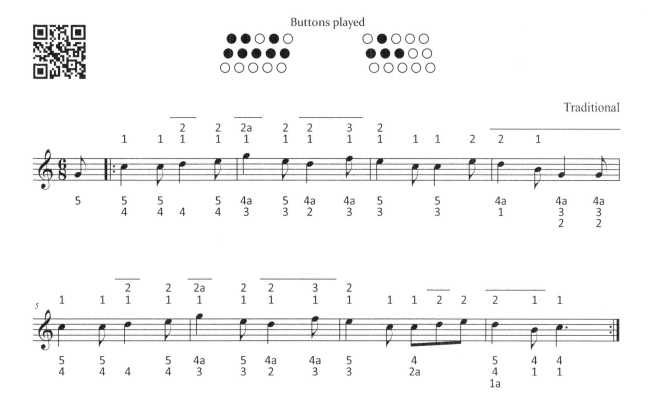

Traditional

Jockey to the Fair

(Ascot-under-Wychwood)

AABCB

Buttons played

Traditional

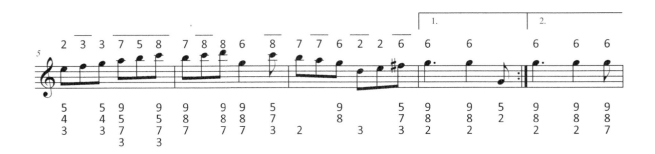

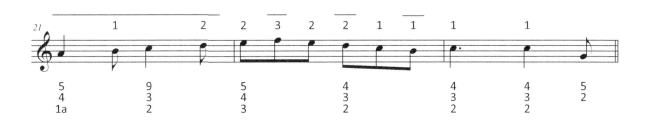

Johnny Come Down to Hilo

Buttons played

Traditional

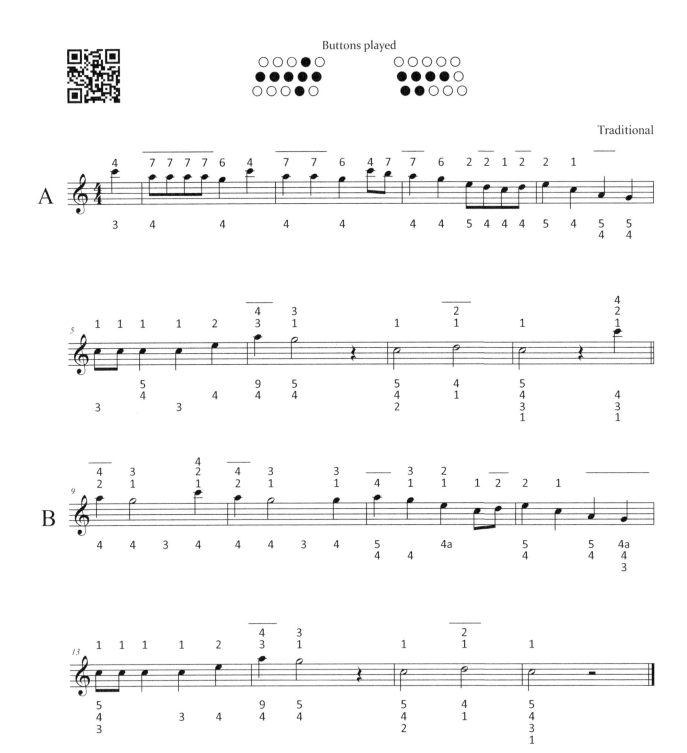

THE KEEL ROW

Buttons played

Traditional

A

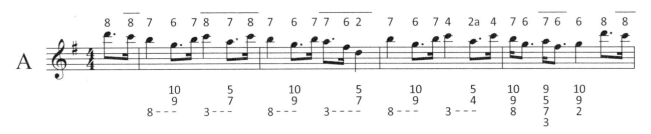

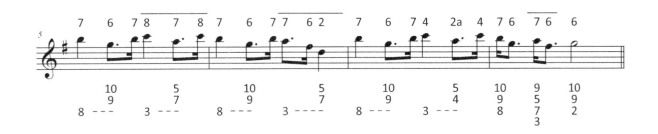

B

The Anglo Concertina Music of Phil Ham

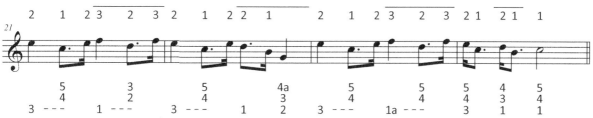

Lads-a-Bunchum

(Adderbury)

Buttons played

Traditional

MAID OF THE MILL

(Bampton)

Buttons played

Traditional

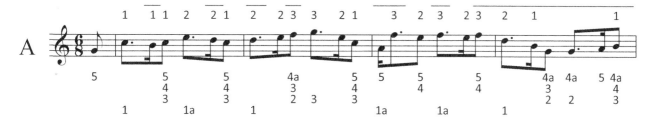

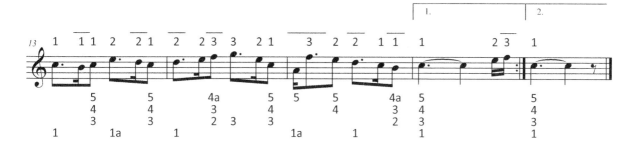

Tunes for a Maypole Dance

Buttons played

Boys & Girls Come Out to Play

Traditional

A

B

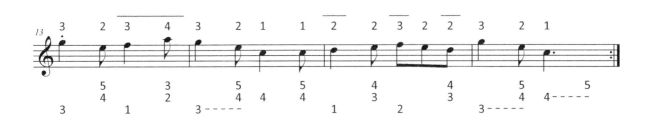

Boys & Girls Come Out to Play (slow)

Here We Go 'Round the Mulberry Bush

Traditional

For He's a Jolly Good Fellow

Traditional

Milley's Bequest

(Lichfield)

Buttons played

Traditional

A

B

Monk's March

(Sherborne)

Buttons played

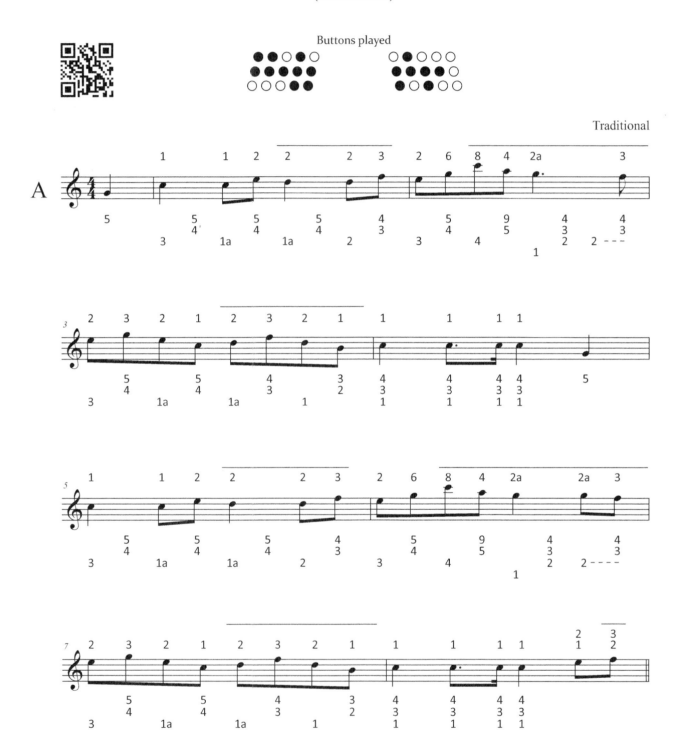

Traditional

The Anglo Concertina Music of Phil Ham

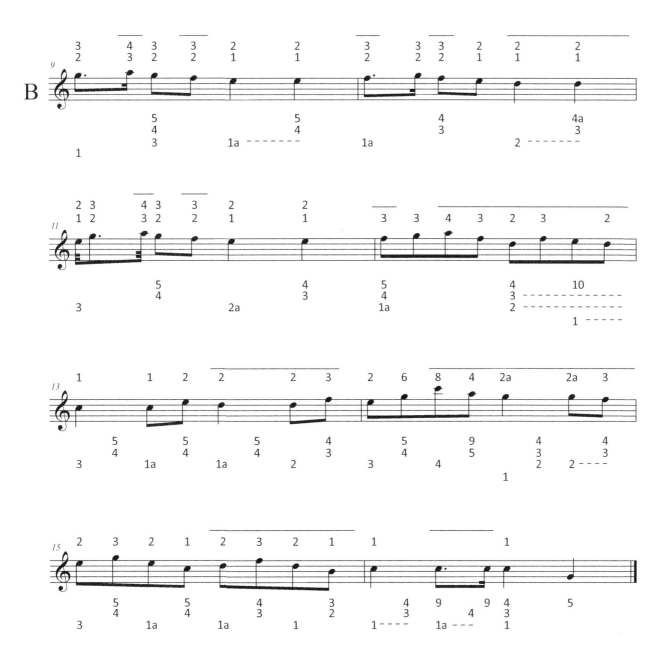

Mrs Casey

(Ascot-under-Wychwood)

Traditional

The Anglo Concertina Music of Phil Ham

Mrs Casey

(Field Town)

Buttons played

Traditional

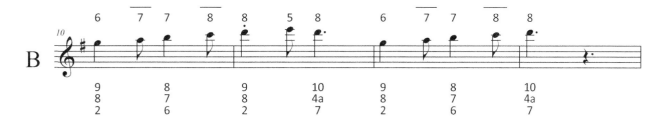

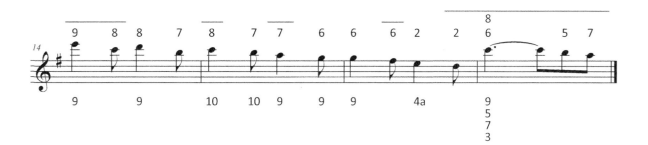

None So Pretty

(Field Town)

Traditional

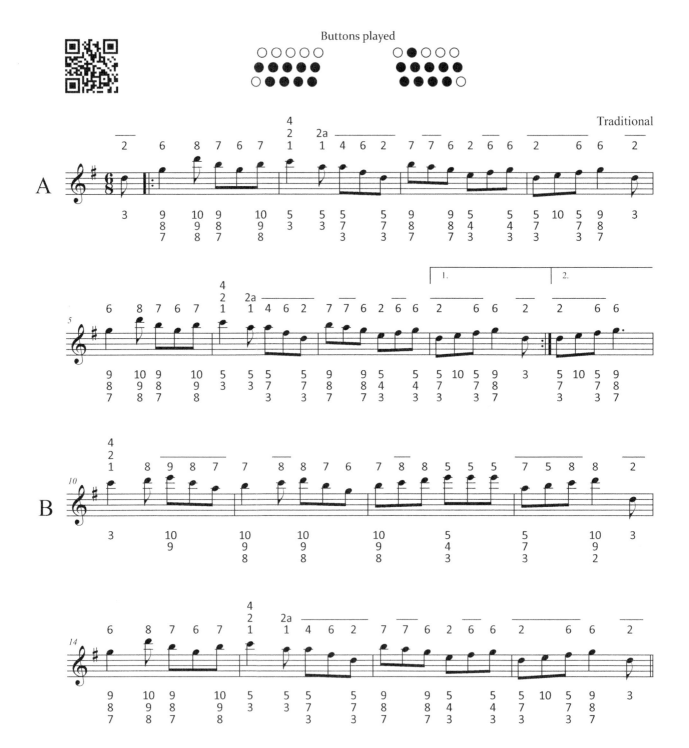

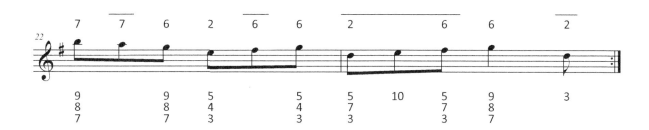

NOW IS THE MONTH OF MAYING

Traditional

The Anglo Concertina Music of Phil Ham

The Anglo Concertina Music of Phil Ham

The Nutting Girl

(Bampton)

Buttons played

Traditional

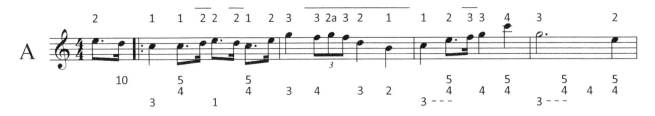

On Ilkley Moor Baht'At

Buttons played

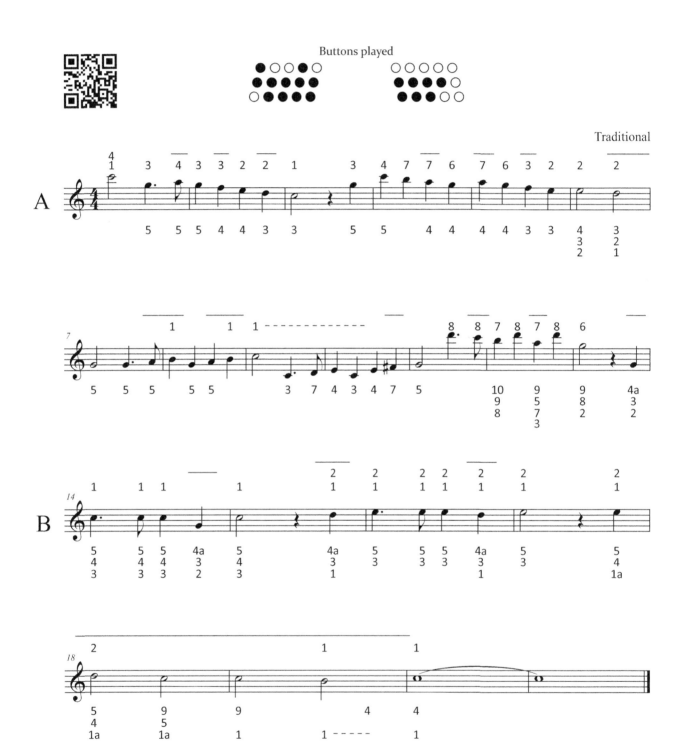

The Anglo Concertina Music of Phil Ham

Princess Royal

(Abingdon)

Buttons played

Traditional

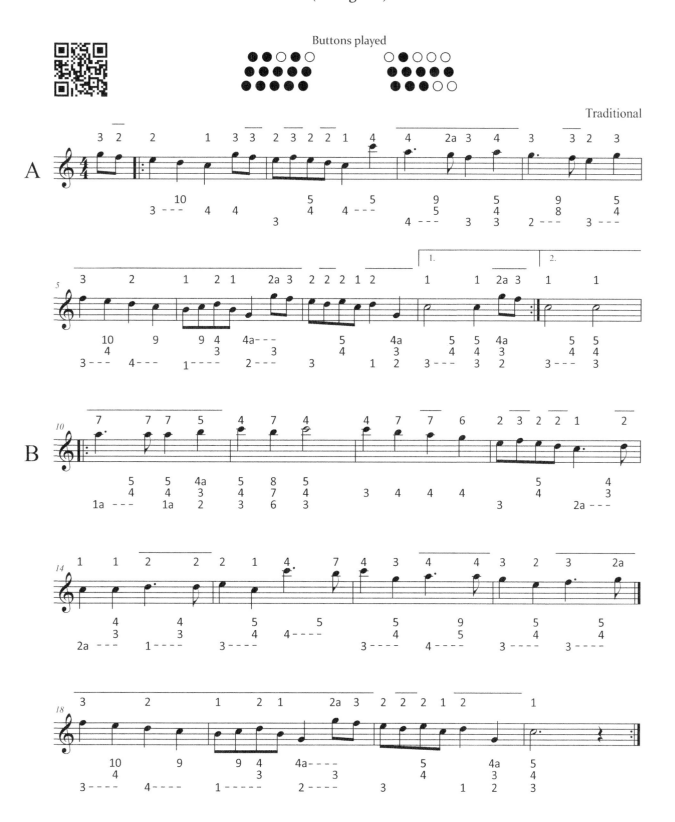

The Quaker

(Bampton)

Buttons played

Traditional

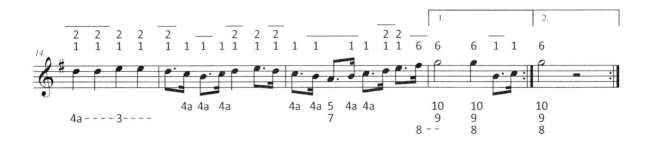

RODNEY

(Headington)

Buttons played

Traditional

The Rose

(Field Town)
AABBCCBB

Buttons played

Traditional

A

B

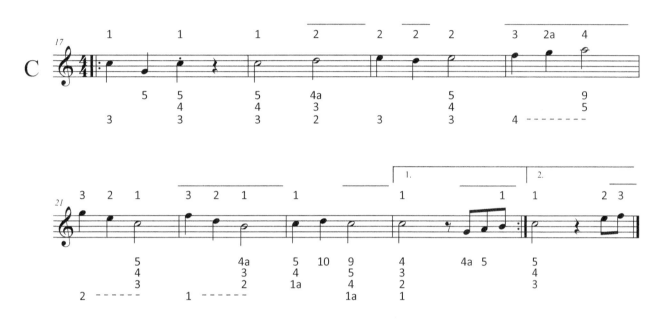

Santy Anna

Buttons played

Traditional

Shenandoah

Buttons played

Traditional

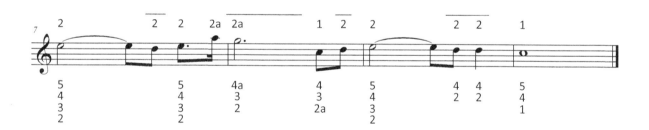

Sheriff's Ride

(Lichfield)

Buttons played

Traditional

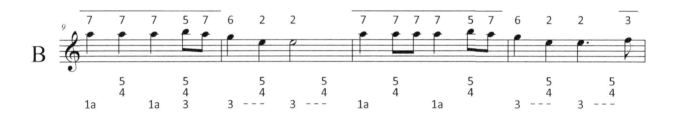

The Anglo Concertina Music of Phil Ham

Since First I Saw Your Face

Buttons played

Thomas Ford (1607)

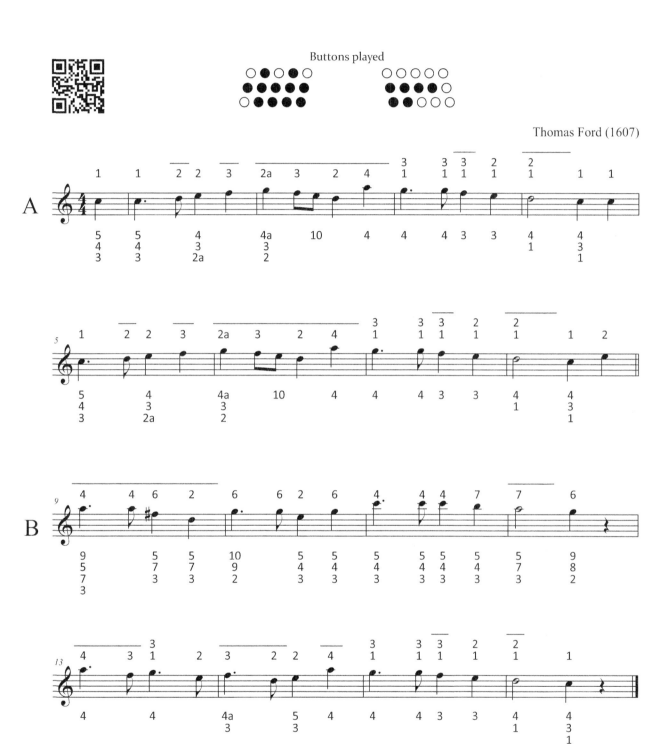

Strike it Up, Tabor

Buttons played

Thomas Weelkes (1608)

Trumpet Tune in D

Buttons played

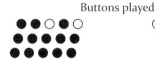

Jeremiah Clarke (1699)

A

B

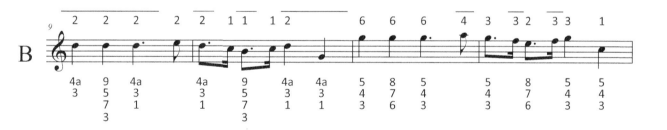

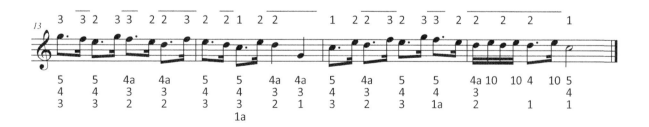

TRUNKLES

(Headington)

A(A2B3C3)2A2B3D3

Buttons played

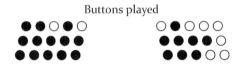

Traditional

A

B

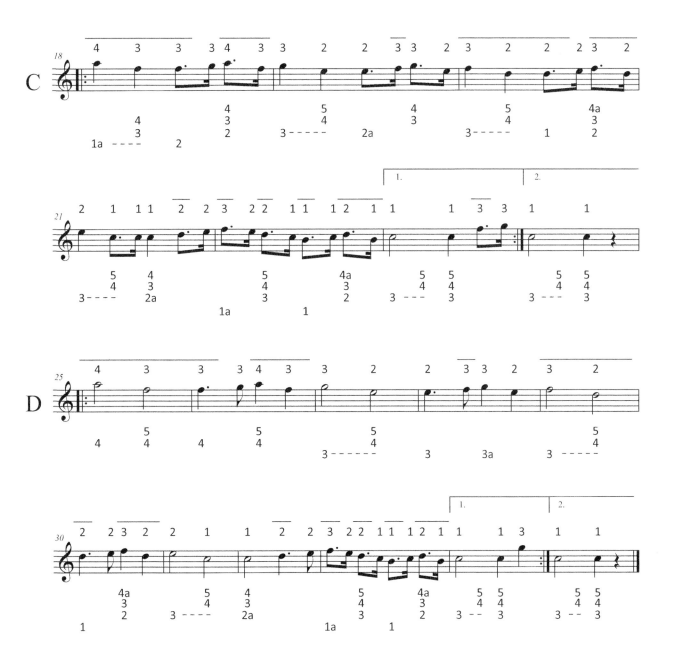

Twenty-Ninth of May

(Headington)

Buttons played

Traditional

A

B

Valentine

(Ascot-under-Wychwood)

Buttons played

Traditional

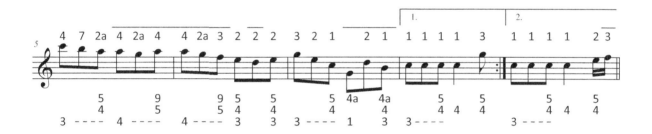

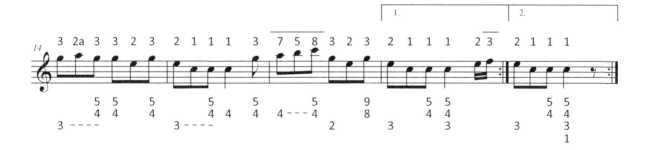

The Vandalls of Hammerwich

(Lichfield)

Buttons played

Traditional

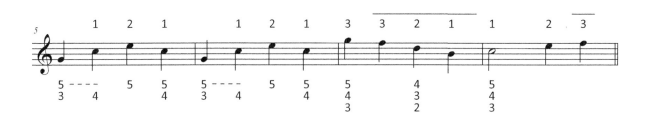

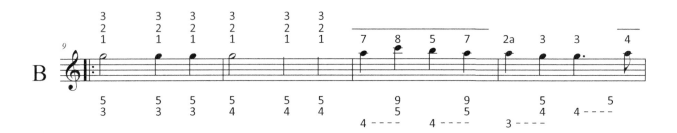

The Vicar of Bray

Buttons played

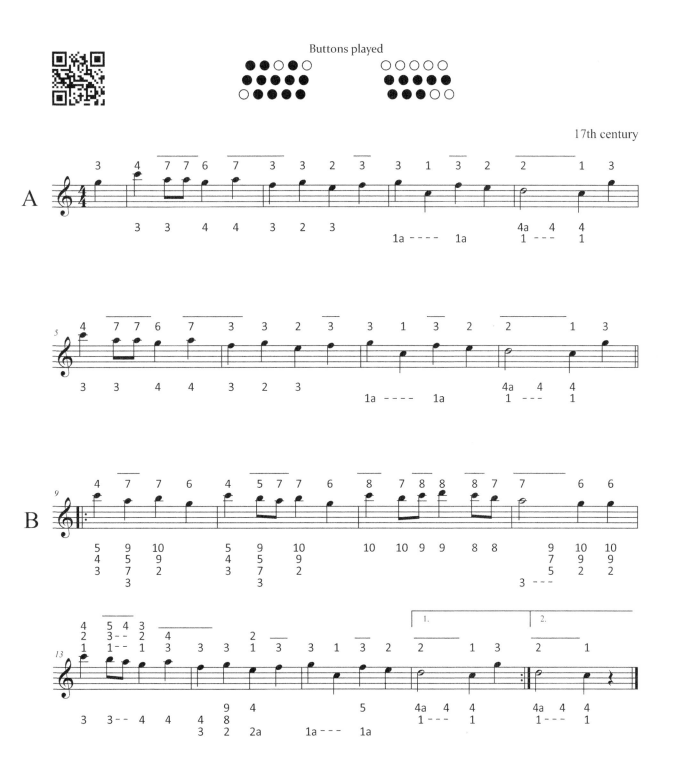

17th century

William & Nancy

(Bledington)

Buttons played

Traditional

A

B

The Anglo Concertina Music of Phil Ham

C

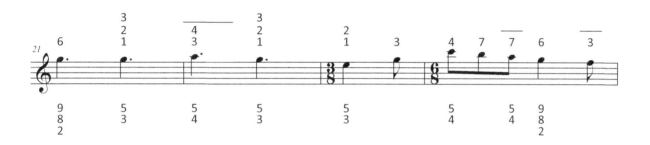

Notes on the Tunes

Here are a few lines of comment for each of the tunes:

A Great and Mighty Wonder

This may be the first tune in the book but it's not the best one to start on.

But when you feel you are ready, play the recording over several times and make sure you know the tune and are on the way to memorising it. Then play it a few more times and listen to the chords and see if you can recognise and then repeat them on your own instrument. Then put the two together – but never wait too long to do so.

A-Roving (Sea Shanty)

I usually play the Shantyman's verse as a solo line or in octaves, and then play the response in harmony. The Victorian collectors of such pieces found themselves quite unable to print most of the known verses as they were thought to be too rude.

Bacca Pipes (Ascot-under-Wychwood)

Strictly speaking, separate A and B sections are needed for this dance, but the ones known are unfortunately exactly the same, so we need to make them sound a bit different. English Bacca Pipe dances are related to the Scottish Sword dances, but with a pair of long clay "Churchwarden pipes" crossed on the floor; if you step on one it will break. It has been said that the length of these pipes enabled a Church Warden to hang the bowl out of the Church window during a lengthy sermon and pass the time with a smoke.

Bacca Pipes (Headington – 4th Tune Variant)

This dance is similar to the Ascot-under-Wychwood and other dances of the same name. The Headington tune (of which there are four variants) is played in D minor (based on the C row). A bit of a challenge but a very nice tune.

Balance the Straw (Field Town)

The Field Town dances are "more graceful but less powerful than most – which calls for strong phrasing". This version is not to be found in the usual references however, having "appeared" after WW2. It is a "long-stick" dance similar to Young Collins.

BALANCY STRAW (ASCOT-UNDER-WYCHWOOD)

A similar dance to the Field Town dance with almost the same name; in both dances the stick-tapping sections are played in octaves, rather than harmonically, to give extra emphasis. Whilst this dance is scored in 4/4 time, the Field Town one is in more conventional 6/8 time. (And it doesn't seem to make much difference!)

BANBURY BILL (BAMPTON)

The last three bars of the A Music of this tune have been transposed down an octave to make it easier/possible to play. Much of the A Music is written in the "oom-pa" style of ("bass note – chord – bass" etc.) but the B Music is varied with a kind of "intermittent duet" style as a contrast to the A Music.

THE BANKS OF THE DEE (FIELD TOWN)

The first two notes of the tune must be played by the left hand whilst it is also playing the accompaniment; not difficult once you have got used to the idea. Playing in thirds in the 3rd bar of the B music is also easy, but for the last three notes of that bar the top C in the G row is played using the little (or 5th) finger, with Pull all the way, to help the phrasing.

BEAUX OF LONDON CITY (BADBY)

A Tradition with very few dances, the best-known of which is The Beaux of London City. I have played this one with mostly block chords. It is probably one of the easier ones to start on for that reason – but listen to (and learn) the melody first.

BILLY BOY (LOCAL NORTHUMBRIAN SONG)

Billy Boy is quite a robust Northumbrian tune and quite a suitable one to try when you have had some experience of a few Morris Dances. It has a few alternative styles of harmonisation in it and other useful tricks to try, including octaves, sixths, block chords, etc. This tune has been used for a Sea Shanty as well.

THE BLACK JOKE (ILMINGTON)

Although this dance is best known as a "Hand-Clapping dance" with a normal Morris-Step, there are options to use Sticks or Handkerchiefs. In the usual form, the dance finishes with opposites touching palms; the tune is a particular favourite. To get that nice little discord (which is part of the Chord) on the first note of the second bar you will, on a 30-key instrument, need to play a C on Pull from the G row in the Left Hand.

BLAYDON RACES (LOCAL NORTHUMBRIAN SONG)

This Newcastle Anthem was written for champion rower and boat-builder Harry Clasper; when he died in 1870 more than 130,000 people lined the streets to pay tribute. The 'A' music taps out the story with block chords (reminiscent of modern Rap) played staccato; the 'B' Chorus music includes a few bars of 'oom-pa' style and ends with the words: "to see the Blaydon Races!"

BLOW THE MAN DOWN (SEA SHANTY)

The repeats hint at the ways you might vary the music to match some of the words.

THE BLUEBELLS OF SCOTLAND (SCOTTISH AIR)

This is a tune which requires the little finger of your right hand to get up to the high C in the G row all in the same run (e.g. as in the 2nd bar of the A Music). It is a rather sad song – not actually about flowers but the Blue Bell pub where the 'Bonny Lad' lived before he was sent off to the war, and from which he has never returned.

BOBBING AROUND (BAMPTON)

Several variants have been unearthed by later collectors who have revisited Bampton. The two prominent chords in the 'B' music correspond to when the dancers are jumping high in a Caper movement.

BOBBY SHAFTOE (TRADITIONAL NORTHUMBRIAN TUNE)

This tune in C is quite easy and a good one to start on. The recording first gives you the melody and then repeats it with various styles of accompaniment. You can also play the same things on the 'G' row (but the fingering is not exactly the same).

BOUND FOR THE RIO GRANDE (SEA SHANTY)

This tune gives the Shantyman's verse as single notes or octaves, followed by the response in the Harmonic style. Variants of this tune "are legion" but this is one of the best.

COUNTRY GARDENS (FIELD TOWN)

A popular tune, thanks to well-known orchestral versions. The tune stays within the octave but the phrasing is helped if the top B is taken on Pull from the G row.

DEAREST DICKY (FIELD TOWN)

This is perhaps the best tune from all the Field Town collection. It runs briskly up and down the scale and gets even more drive from the staccato chords in the bass. It would be possible to use easier chords than noted here for the Capers, but the ones on the recording add interest.

DOUBLE LEAD THROUGH (HEADINGTON FOLK DANCE)

A rumbustious folk-dance from Headington Quarry which needs all the punch you can get from the inherent push/pull of the Anglo. Play the chords with a staccato touch for this tune – but use no more than three buttons or you may drown the melody. The Article from 1965 shows the chords available.

THE DRESSED SHIP (PLAYFORD DANCE, CA. 1650)

Like all Playford Dances this tune should flow along gracefully in true Harmonic style. You will need always to choose whatever buttons will give you a Push or Pull for the Tune which will match the chord you will be using in the left hand.

DRUNKEN SAILOR (SEA SHANTY)

This tune needs to be played very crisply. It is played on the G row but is actually in E minor. Only three 3-note chords are needed for the whole tune.

FINE KNACKS FOR LADIES (DOWLAND, 1600)

The original tune for this Madrigal is set in perfect four-part harmony – but the recording is not quite so strict. The three lower parts tend to move about while the "Soprano" voice (the Tune) has a Rest; these lower parts are not part of the melody. The sub-plot in the words is that the travelling pedlar is also a part-time gigolo, hence the Chorus: "Though all my wares be Trash/ The heart is True! / The heart is True!"

FIRE DOWN BELOW (SEA SHANTY)

In the Chorus to it is helpful to make use of the G on Pull in the top row of keys. This enables you to play the triplets in the 3rd bar of the B music all on Pull in order to match the bass chord.

GETTING UPSTAIRS (HEADINGTON)

This is one of the many Headington dances in 2/2 or 4/4 time. All Headington dances should be played crisply; some musicians help this feeling by playing some of the notes in the Melody as if dotted, and the block chords very staccato.

GEUD MAN OF BALLANGIGH (PLAYFORD DANCE, CA. 1650)

Like all Playford Dances this tune should flow along gracefully in true Harmonic style. You will need always to choose whatever buttons will give you a Push or Pull for the Tune which will match the chord you will be using in the left hand.

HANDKERCHIEF DANCE (UPTON-UPON-SEVERN)

This is a nice tune; it is set in C major but wanders in and out of A minor – which is rather attractive. Unfortunately, there is not enough information to describe the dance so it is never performed.

HERE'S TO THE MAIDEN (TRADITIONAL ENGLISH SONG)

"Here's to the Maiden of Bashful Fifteen; Here's to the widow of fifty; Here's to the Flaunting extravagant quean, And here's to the housewife that's thrifty". It is basically a drinking song, and there are many varieties of the tune. In playing it, full advantage should be taken of the alternative notes in the right hand.

HIGHLAND MARY (ASCOT-UNDER-WYCHWOOD)

A quite jolly tune in G Major and played on the G row with occasional borrowing from the C row. The chords are relatively easy, so suitable for a relative beginner.

HUNTING THE SQUIRREL (HEADINGTON)

Commonly known as 'Hunt the Squirrel' this is a fairly easy piece; it is played all on the C row for the A Music, but then using the G row for two chords in the B Music.

One for a relative beginner.

I SAW THREE SHIPS (ENGLISH CHRISTMAS CAROL)

This tune should bounce along gently and happily. Basically, the harmonies in the first line of music are alternate C and G chords, with the odd A Minor thrown in towards the end. For words like: "And now we all with one accord ... " you might play a few bars in octaves to suggest unity.

JOCKEY TO THE FAIR (ASCOT-UNDER-WYCHWOOD)

A tune found in many traditions, and played here in octaves interspersed with passages played in the Harmonic style. A short, solo Jig (for one dancer).

JOHNNY COME DOWN TO HILO (SEA SHANTY)

Sea Shanties are not all loud and fast; this one is fairly easy and played with different degrees of expression for each Repeat – perhaps to suit different verses.

THE KEEL ROW (TRADITIONAL NORTHUMBRIAN SONG)

Played first in G and then in C, this song is about a "lassie" who sang of her "laddie" who was due to come home on a Keel – a boat-of-all-trades working on the River Tyne. A good one for mastering a range of Chords for the Harmonic style.

LADS-A-BUNCHUM (ADDERBURY)

A Stick-tapping Dance with a fairly easy tune to play. The sharp chords in the B music denote when the sticks clash. It starts with a Walk-Around with the Side singing: Oh! dear mother, what a fool I be; / Six young fellows came a-courting me. / Three are blind and the others can't see. / Oh! dear mother, what a fool I be!

MAID OF THE MILL (BAMPTON)

The Bampton dancers "danced with verve, stepping briskly." The tune (which is fairly straightforward) should reflect this characteristic. I don't apologise for going up to E instead of C in the first bar of the B music – it suits the concertina better!

MAYPOLE DANCE TUNES (TRADITIONAL)

This is a small selection of tunes which I have used for children dancing one or two of the easy figures in a Maypole Dance. They would be ideal for a beginner on the Anglo Concertina to start on; they can be played on the C row or the G row.

MILLEY'S BEQUEST (LICHFIELD)

A Two-stick dance in the North-West Morris Dance tradition. It is associated with performing in streets paved with stone 'setts' by dancers wearing traditional wooden 'cloggs' – perhaps fitted with iron toe and heel caps, which exceeded Morris-bells for noise. Note the use of consecutive thirds to beef up the tune in the B music.

MONKS' MARCH (SHERBORNE)

A straightforward, swaggering tune in C major for a "Hand-Clapping" dance. It is also one of those using a "Heel-and-Toe" step (and probably the best known one). Note the use of consecutive thirds in the tune of the B Music – this is a very useful technique to practice.

MRS CASEY (ASCOT-UNDER-WYCHWOOD)

A cheerful tune for a fairly vigorous stick dance; the A music uses an "oom-pa" style whilst the B Music mostly has block chords for the stick-clashing. Not too difficult.

MRS CASEY (FIELD TOWN)

This tune is for another "Heel-and-Toe" dance very similar to Monk's March (although the stepping is not quite the same). The rather haunting (but easy) A Music is mostly in the key of A minor but manages to get back into the key of C major in the last couple of bars. The B Music is all in C major and accompanies hand movements as in Monk's March. Well worth a try.

NONE SO PRETTY (FIELD TOWN)

A "Hand-Clapping" dance but with a normal Morris 4-step rather than a "Heel-and-Toe" step. A cheerful tune, which hops lightly about the keyboard, accompanied by block chords in the A and B music. The first passage in the C music is played in Octaves, ending with a couple of bars using block chords. Worth playing for the variety.

NOW IS THE MONTH OF MAYING (THOMAS MORLEY, 1595)

A Madrigal traditionally sung on the tops of towers by students to usher in the 1st of May. Written in 5-part harmony, it is played here in (almost) 4-parts. Must be played very briskly and with expression. With a few words of persuasion, the singers invite "Dainty Nymphs" to play "Barley Break" with them in the fields. (Well, that's one way of putting it.)

THE NUTTING GIRL (BAMPTON)

A happy Folk- tune for a straightforward dance. Collected with a few added trills, grace-notes etc., and a few more have been included since. It is played generally in the Harmonic style, and there are a few places where other tricks have been included – such as octaves, falling or rising passages in the bass, etc., to provide interest to the arrangement.

ON ILKLEY MOOR BAHT 'AT (YORKSHIRE DIALECT SONG)

In plain English: "On Ilkley Moor Without a Hat" – the answer to the opening question (and also repeated as a Chorus after each verse). "Wheear hast tha been sin' I saw thee? / On Ilkley Moor baht "at / Tha'll go and get thi deeath o' cowld! / Then we shall ha' to bury thee / Then t' worms 'll come 'an ate thee oop / Then t' ducks 'll come a' ate t' worms / Then we shall go an' ate t' ducks / Then we shall all 'ave eaten thee!" The recording is an accompaniment, and an echo of the spontaneous but lusty harmonisation of Yorkshire singers.

PRINCESS ROYAL (ABINGDON)

One of the best tunes in the book, versions of which are performed by many Morris sides. It may have originated from "Miss MacDermott or The Princess Royal" by the Irish Harpist Carolan, then used a few years later as: "The Arethusa" in "The Lock and Key" at the Drury Lane Theatre in London before being carried round England by itinerant musicians and picked up by the locals.

THE QUAKER (BAMPTON)

This tune does not fit in very well to the compass of a 30-key Anglo, hence for the A music it has been set in the key of C major using a "close harmony" style. The B music can then be played on the G row of keys, mostly making much use of consecutive thirds.

RODNEY (HEADINGTON)

A dance in the typical Headington style: crisp and fairly fast. It is virtually essential to "borrow" chords from the G row in both the Right and Left hands – particularly in the B music.

THE ROSE (FIELD TOWN)

Another fine (and not particularly difficult) tune for quite a short dance. The dancers must get themselves ready to go straight into the first Figure: Rounds. Other Figures follow; hardly drawing breath. The musician has to be awake, too.

SANTY ANNA (SEA SHANTY)

A slightly sombre tune which benefits from not being played too fast. It is set in the key of D minor, but don't be alarmed – just use the C row and mentally reverse all the Push/Pulls, when you will find yourself in D minor and it gets quite easy.

SHENANDOAH (SEA SHANTY)

An easy tune in C major; it is best to have the Shantyman's calls as solo tunes and the responses in Harmonic Style.

SHERRIFF'S RIDE (LICHFIELD)

A Single-stick dance in the North-west Morris Tradition, which has eight dancers rather than the six of the many Cotswold Traditions. Instead of a "Once-to-Yourself" Lichfield dances start straight in with one or two Chords.

SINCE FIRST I SAW YOUR FACE (THOMAS FORD, 1607)

Although regarded as a Madrigal, this tune is really a charming Love-song set in four parts. Play the tune with expression and gently add the appropriate 3-note Chords with the left hand. This song was in continuous publication right up to 1920/30.

STRIKE IT UP, TABOR (THOMAS WEELKES. 1607)

The Verse is best played as a kind of duet; to play the fast runs at the end of each Chorus you need to play it all on Pull and find all the notes you need to complete the scale. The words to this Madrigal are virtually incomprehensible!

TRUMPET TUNE IN D (JEREMIAH CLARKE 1699)

You need to be familiar with all the chords in the Left-hand to play this one; it can also be difficult to avoid the chords (standing in for a pipe organ) from overwhelming the melody.

TRUNKLES (HEADINGTON)

A lively Headington Stick dance, which is best done in the shortened version. Not difficult, but the musician needs to watch out for the stick-clashing and play the accompanying chords at the same time.

THE TWENTY-NINTH OF MAY (HEADINGTON)

A lively Headington Handkerchief dance. Relatively easy but – like all Headington – fast.

VALENTINE (ASCOT-UNDER-WYCHWOOD)

The attractive tune for this Handkerchief dance covers a fair bit of ground, but the accompaniment is quite easy.

VANDALLS OF HAMMERWICH (LICHFIELD)

A relatively stately Long-Stick dance, and notable for the vigour with which the sticks are clashed. The dances were also used as processionals, pausing occasionally to stop and perform a complete dance. Not difficult.

The Vicar of Bray (Satirical English Song)

This "Broadsheet Ballad" tells of the era 1660 to 1714 when five successive Monarchs held the British Throne – each having an opposite religious persuasion to the previous one. Many Churchmen were deprived of their Livings on most of these occasions – but not the Vicar of Bray, who found no difficulty in making adjustments.

The tune is harmonised using various techniques, from duet to block chords, consecutive sixths and brief periods of four-part harmony. Well worth a try.

William and Nancy (Bledington)

Quite a lively Handkerchief Dance, with some "oom-pa" style accompaniment interspersed with octaves, block chords and flashes of duet. If you have managed most of the others, this one should be a walk in the park (as they say).

Phil Ham

My Journey with the Anglo Concertina

Phil Ham

When people ask "How did you learn to play the concertina?" I usually say "I really don't know; it was a long time ago." But a Christmas present from my parents when I was about five or six was a mouth-organ, and I quickly grasped the principle of blow/suck to play a scale and make tunes. This happens to be virtually the same as the Anglo concertina keyboard, so that when I later got an Anglo it seemed instantly familiar. I also had lessons on the piano, and learned a lot but didn't really take to it at the time.

Every Sunday afternoon from the age of about six I was packed off to the Congregational Sunday School less than a mile down the road. This, like many other things to do with the Chapel, was organized by a Mr. Clarredge, whose pitch-free corncrake voice led every hymn and expounded on every piece of scripture as required.

My association with the Chapel came with a lot of singing over the years, and I seemed naturally to absorb the basic principles of harmony – not only during services but also at outings of various kinds where spontaneous community singing could always break out. And, when you were older, there was the Youth Club which was held every Friday Night in the Old Chapel across the road. Inside there was warmth, badminton in the large hall, and table tennis in the smaller room. There was also a piano for anyone who wanted to play it and an old wind-up portable gramophone with assorted 78 records. The very thought brings to mind the experience of playing badminton to the distant tune of "The Sugar Plum Fairy."

At the Youth Club I met Leslie Curtis who very good on the piano but even better on his accordion. In order to show me a bit more of the accordion, he invited me a few times into the back rooms of "The Denmark Inn" where his grandparents were the licensees, but the pub was effectively run by his grandmother and his father, who happened to own an English Concertina although I was never lucky enough to hear him play it. The grandfather did very little in the pub, but did play a 20-key Anglo concertina.

I was able to try this rather basic instrument, but every time I did so he would light up and say: "Ah! I know the one you are trying to play" and would then play something unrecognisable. The experience of the instrument was very interesting and gave me encouragement to look out for one. Not very long afterwards, I spotted an old wooden-ended 26-key Jones concertina in a second-hand shop window for the price of £1:17/6d. (about £1.87 in modern money but think in terms of around £80 now) It took me many frugal weeks to save up the cash and then I went right in and bought it.

The bellows leaked and it was generally scruffy and rather wheezy. However, Woolworth's sold thin leather patches with which to mend your coat elbows and a few of those allowed me to make neat little corners for all the bellows. So, after a bit of a general clean-up I had a functioning musical instrument. Only a few months later I could confidently hold forth on *Ten Green Bottles, She'll be Coming Round the Mountain* and various other such stalwarts.

It was two or three years later that I got my first real inspiration for the Anglo concertina. In Town one Saturday morning I heard the unmistakable sound of a concertina being played quite loudly some way off. Looking for where it came from, I saw an upright but somewhat shabbily dressed man with close-cropped grey hair who was holding his Anglo at head-height and playing what I later found out was "Trumpet Tune" by Jeremiah Clark! He was playing very well but seemed to be blind, for he was making his way slowly along with one foot in the gutter and the other on the pavement. I was quite bowled over, and followed him for about five minutes at a respectful distance. I can still see and hear him in my mind's eye right now.

My life soon changed quite suddenly at the age of fifteen; I was diagnosed with a spinal condition which kept me at home for a year. At the end of it I was even more competent at the concertina but had to give up playing the piano for the time being. But thankfully I had learned how to study on my own, so that when I returned to formal education was able to win a scholarship to study Engineering. Virtually my only recreation at University was the *Bristol University Choral Society* led by Prof. W. K. Stanton.

They met in the largest lecture theatre in the Physics Building; there were no auditions or anything of that kind, and attendance turned out to be a very pleasant mixture of relaxation and hard work. Then at the beginning of the second Term we learned that the end-of-year performance would be of Vaughan William's *Sea Symphony*. Prof. Stanton read out the letter that he had received from the composer wishing us "*all success in your performance of my hateful Work,*" which seemed an unusual comment to make. In subsequent decades RVW gained much success with his Works based on the many Folk songs he had collected (eight hundred?) as well as themes from other composers.

The next year our main production was Beethoven's Mass in C, a challenging Work which we performed with some success in Bristol Cathedral. In the third and final year we practised for a choral work by Gustav Holst which involved some difficult passages for unaccompanied choir. Unfortunately, many people who had heard that the performance was to be recorded for BBC Radio turned up on the day without having attended many (if any) of the practices. When the orchestra re-entered after the final unaccompanied section, the choir had dropped a whole tone, and the ending sounded terrible. As the last notes died away, poor Prof. Stanton slumped like a broken man. The BBC Singers (all sixteen of them) filled in for the broadcast performance a week or two later. Therein lies a lesson on the benefits of adequate practice

The Anglo Concertina Music of Phil Ham

In my last year the idea of the Bristol University Choral Society having a float in the annual Rag Procession gained some traction. Peter Pugsley, Marcus Beer and I were persuaded to "do something." Marcus could already play a saxophone, Peter could play a Recorder but found a clarinet from somewhere, and I had an old clarinet which I had bought for £5 in one of Bristol's street markets. I took it home in the second-year vacation and fixed various small defects. Back at Bristol with it I could play a small selection of tunes in B flat so we had the makings of a Band, and it all worked quite well. It was nothing to do with singing; nothing to do with the Anglo, but a good fun musical experience.

My three years at University came to an end, and I chose a job offer from GEC at Stanmore in the North-London suburbs. By sheer luck, within weeks of my arrival I had found an advertisement in the local press for singers to join a new small choir being put together to perform part-songs, madrigals and a small amount of liturgical music. So began another phase of my musical life, but the concertina had to wait just a little bit longer before I could resurrect it – as living in lodgings hardly allowed for practice.

As a member of the *Allegro Singers*, who were centred on the choir of St. Albans Parish Church in Golders Green, I automatically entered the Church choir and – being on the outskirts of London – was within reach of an enveloping swirl of varied musical opportunities, either as a listener or a performer. But, whilst these various musical experiences were both variegated and enjoyable, I soon came to realise that I could not continue long-term with many of them due to the difficulty of getting in and out of Town on time. There were unexpected hazards as well: I can hardly forget the Great London Smog of 1952 when I had to walk from Edgeware Tube Station late at night to Mrs. Geiger's lodgings half a mile away. Quite apart from the choking atmosphere, it was almost impossible to see one's feet even when standing under a street lamp. But I remembered the blind Anglo Concertina player in Taunton and proceeded slowly through the smothering silence with one foot in the gutter until, with enormous relief, I eventually reached the front door.

It is said that "all good things come to an end" and although I had had some wonderful experiences in my few years with the Allegro Singers, the end arrived fairly quickly. The leader of the group – Bill Miller – was a dashing but jobless graduate who had just come down from Oxford but after a few months he obtained a Management place with the Pfizer Corporation, who were setting up a facility in Sandwich. Within three years Bill had to move to Sandwich permanently (and, eventually, the USA for a dazzling career) and could not continue to lead the Singers. That was just about the time that I had become fed up with living in lodgings and set about buying a house up in Stanmore.

With this housing move I was finally able to bring my 26-key Anglo concertina up from Somerset and start serious playing again. It was another stroke of luck that Peter Pugsley turned up in Stanmore, too. He invited me to go along to the Circassian Circle Folk-Dance Club (CCC) which, at that time, was meeting in a hall in Stanmore village every week. Folk-dancing supplanted singing surprisingly quickly and became my main leisure activity for the next few years.

There were some occasions on which a few of the group visited Cecil Sharp House, the headquarters of *The English Folk Dance and Song Society* (EFDSS). On one such visit I saw a Morris Dance being performed for the first time; it was "The Queen's Delight" from Bucknell. I don't remember where the team came from, but the musician was Brian Heaton on a large "Shand" melodeon. (He still plays for the West Somerset Morris Men!) After this introduction I went home and worked the out the melody and accompaniment on my 26-key Anglo. A very nice tune but, unfortunately, I was rarely able to play it as none of the Teams I played for normally did the Bucknell dances.

The CCC was also invited a few times to take part in the annual EFDSS "National Gathering" performances in the Albert Hall in London. This, predictably, required practices at Cecil Sharp House, which were run with a rod of iron by a few middle-aged ladies who had the psychological advantage of having known Cecil Sharp (though not in the Biblical sense, I hasten to add). At one of these sessions work was suddenly interrupted by the presence of Vaughan Williams in person, who proceeded to lecture us on what to do if we ever encountered some original folk-song material. This turned out to be absolutely nothing: no collecting, no performing, no recording; and above all – no passing it on. We should get in touch with a "Qualified Folk-Song Collector" and leave it to him/her. Aural transmission – as practiced by traditional singers over the Centuries was forbidden. I was not at all impressed by this vision of the prescribed future for Folk Music.

In late summer 1959 the Club made a two-week visit to Germany, where I played my concertina for the one or two men who could dance Morris Jigs. During the first week we visited and performed in Cologne, Hannover, Goslar, Braunschweig, and Bad Harzburg, as well as meeting other dancers, musicians and Bandoneon groups. For the second week, by way of relaxation, we were taken to a camping hut in the Harz Mountains. The scenery was beautiful but the accommodation was very frugal.

All our performances on the visit to Germany had gone very well, and I played for the Jigs as required, but to be on the safe side I used a music-stand with some of Sharp's piano arrangements in front of me. As soon as I got home, I joined The Woodside Morris Men based in North London and resolved that any dances I played for I would only do so from memory and not resort to a music stand; I soon found that I could indeed learn most tunes pretty quickly. How to do the dances took somewhat longer.

I then set about finding a better concertina than the old faithful 26-key Jones. At that time, such a quest would usually involve the weekly publication *Exchange and Mart* (colloquially known as the *Swap and Flog*) in which Tommy Williams advertised fairly regularly. He was, at that time, a bit of a legend so, as soon as I could, I set off for Battersea in South London to find out what he might have for sale.

Arriving at the large Victorian terrace house with Tommy William's small nameplate by the door, I rang the bell and waited. After a short while a woman opened the door and motioned me to go upstairs. I mounted several flights of bare wooden stairs, arrived at the attic room, knocked on the door, and went in. Tommy himself was a very small man with a broad Cockney accent who wore a permanent flat-cap on his head. If he possessed any teeth they must have been elsewhere for the day. Apart from his tools, several concertinas and a jumble of concertina boxes stacked in one corner, it was almost completely bare – except for a few scraps of carpet and a couple of wooden chairs. The attic ran the full width of the house – maybe twenty-five feet in all with a large sloping window to the rear. Below this was his work-bench, where there was a device for tuning reeds. At the furthest end of the attic was a fireplace in front of which was a stove with a pot of glue gently simmering away. On top of the low mantlepiece was nothing but a long sloping pile of tobacco ash, and just to demonstrate how it got there, Tommy took his pipe out of his mouth and tapped it twice against the wall above the mantlepiece.

The only concertina I thought suitable was a well-used Jeffries 38-key C/G instrument, with the gold-leaf decoration and all the bellows-papers blacked out by what I guessed was shoe dye. But I made sure all the keys worked, it was in tune, and there didn't seem to be any air leaks, so I bought it for £7:10s. (£7.50 in decimal coinage but more like £160 in 2022). Of course, if you bought anything significant from Tommy, you found yourself being treated to a "composition" played on a huge McCann Duet. Most of his tunes appeared to be marches, the block chords spelling out the rhythm pretty adequately. I expect the woman downstairs knew most of them pretty well, too.

I took the Jeffries to Harry Crabb & Son for a check-over. Harry and Neville Crabb worked from a small shop in Islington in North London. The access from the front was through a "barn door" that is, a door split in the middle so they only opened the top half for you; there was a small ledge for doing business on, but they would open the bottom half and let you inside if there was a good reason. They told me that that when Charlie Jeffries was alive the Crabb family used to make the fretworked metal ends for him, and the reason they were exactly 6ins. across the flats was because the nickel-silver sheet that they were made from came in that particular width. Harry Crabb & Co. always had been a small, traditional outfit whereas Wheatstone and Lachenal had produced concertinas on a much larger scale.

My Jeffries instrument lasted me another 24 years before the presence of green mould meant that I had to get a full refurbishment, with completely new bellows (incredible value at £90.00) from Colin Dipper. Alas, the Crabb establishment disappeared round about that time, as Neville had died prematurely and there was no-one else to carry on. Although the Jeffries came from Tommy with the original six-sided leather case, it was rather battered, so I soon found quite a nice square leather case which had at one time held a Wheatstone "Triumph Duet." When I acquired it there was a quite old, but still functional, English concertina inside – probably only worth a pound or two at the time. It didn't sound much like the Jeffries either for, as Tommy Williams said: "Jeffries made the best Anglos wot there ever was." Over the next few years I acquired a few more concertinas – one of which was a huge 77-key Bflat Jeffries Duet – mostly for no better reason than that they were so cheap.

The Woodside Morris Men were a revival side formed in the early 1930s, and they met for practices in a school hall in Finchley, North London; they were mostly taught by Bert Cleaver, later Squire of the Morris Ring. Just a few months before I joined, so did Hugh Rippon, who had recently become a staff member of the EFDSS as Public Relations Officer and joint Editor of the Society's Magazine. He left in 1968 to lecture at the Tile Hill College in Coventry; he also authored the Shire Publications' *Discovering English Folk Dance* in 1975. I must say that, with his departure, the EFDSS missed an exceptional opportunity to bring new blood into the organisation.

In the early 1960s Hugh was looking for material for the rather thin EFDSS Magazine, as a result of which my first article for him appeared in March 1963. The second one appeared in September of the same year and arose due to the expected absence from The London Competition Musical Festival of their Folk Music Adjudicator, the Reverend Kenneth Loveless. I had been recommended by Hugh as a substitute for Kenneth, although I had not yet had the pleasure of meeting Ken in person.

There was much to commend in the range and quality the of music played in the various classes, but there was little doubt about the Folk winner, who was none other than Tom Prince – a craggy but mild-mannered blacksmith from the Consett Iron Works a few miles south of Newcastle upon Tyne. I got to know him very well in later years; he played an English Concertina with great flair and, where required, matching volume – as a result of which one small section at the end of his bellows was inclined to blow inside-out with the force of the moment (and he never seemed to notice). I later found out that he invariably won the Folk Music Class whenever he turned up in London. Fortunately, I had not yet moved to Newcastle at that time so the question of possible favouritism did not arise.

The third article I contributed at Hugh's request appeared in April 1965 and was intended to give beginners some help in learning the Anglo Concertina. For the first time, as far as I am aware in a very short article, pictures of chord patterns for the left hand were given as well as some hints about how to go about the whole learning process. In summary, this advised readers to search out and try as much easy music as they could find and, above all, just enjoy playing.

Probably as a result of these articles I was persuaded to hold one or two Workshops for the Anglo Concertina at Cecil Sharp House. These turned out to be of necessity more elementary than I was expecting, as few attendees had actually got very far and some did not yet possess an instrument, but I trust they found it useful. Neil Wayne, known chiefly as a concertina collector (for his futuristic museum project) brought along a miniature English instrument as an example of what he was seeking to acquire. The miniatures were about two-thirds of the size of the standard 48-key instrument, and probably aimed at the music-hall performers.

The Woodside Morris Men were a side of mixed ages, the balance tending towards the more mature (shall we say). One of the latter was Bill Watt, who had been the sales manager for Wheatstone at one time. He told me that they had been taken over recently by Boosey & Hawkes, better known for their brass instruments. He thought it was in the balance whether the famous concertina maker would survive in a corner of the B&H Works if they did not get enough sales. However, two apprentices had been allocated to the manufacture of concertinas and it was hoped that these would secure the future survival of the marque.

This news motivated me with a desire to help the ailing Company, I ordered a new Model 6A, 40-key C/G Anglo at £70.00 and waited. It took six months to arrive and I carefully took it out of its box and gave it a try. There was something distinctly unsatisfactory about it: the bellows were extremely stiff and would make fast playing and any sort of nuances difficult. Worst of all, the tone was quite unlike what I expected. It was thin, tinny and weak. I could not, I felt, take it along to Morris practices and let everyone hear such a thing. I carried on with the Jeffries and, about a year later, I sold the Wheatstone for around £35 to a lady who had been looking for a new Anglo. B&H later gave up on concertinas completely and sold the name to an individual maker who continues to uphold the Wheatstone brand.

With the Woodside Morris Men in the 1960s I learnt both the tunes and the dances – mostly of the Fieldtown Tradition at first but with some dances from other Traditions. The Woodside Men didn't go to many Morris Ring meetings but had started making an annual trip to Deal, in Kent, every year or two. In Deal we stayed at a pub which could accommodate all of us – which was rarely more than eight or nine. We danced at favourable spots in several of the coastal towns

and generally did very well. By virtue of some sleight of hand which I cannot now recall, Cliff Evans soon retired from the post of Bagman and I took over the job and found myself organising future visits to Deal. I was more an aspiring dancer than a musician in those days, for many of the practices were taken by Bert Cleaver (who became Bagman of the Morris Ring some years later) and Bert liked to play the Pipe and Tabor.

After our day of dance around Deal we danced at a few places on our way home on the Sunday and, of course, I wrote letters beforehand to those who might wish to know about it. At about lunch-time on one such Sunday we duly assembled for a show on the grass outside Canterbury Cathedral when I spotted a clerical gentleman – splendidly attired – heading towards us rather quickly. Hanging on to my concertina and shuffling my sheaf of papers, I jumped forward and asserted that we had permission from The Dean and Chapter; to which his instant reply was: "*I am The Dean and Chapter*." Surprise! All was well in the event – he merely wished us to dance in a slightly different place.

Amongst all this activity I shortly received an invitation to give another Anglo Concertina Workshop – this time at a Folk Meeting at the University of Keele. It was to be shared with the

English Concertina player Alf Edwards, who featured on various EP recordings of English Folk Songs from *The Penguin Book of English Folk Song*. He was actually a professional trombone player from one of London's Classical orchestras, and I was very surprised when he placed sheet music on a stand in front of him for absolutely everything he played. As he remarked to me in an aside: "I can't busk; I never busk; I don't play a note without the music."

At Keele I also met Brian Hayden, who was at the time wrestling with the fingering of the Anglo Concertina, and went on later to devise (and patent) his new Duet fingering system in an effort to rationalise the layout and make it easier to play in many keys. This I regard as a bit of a pipe dream as there is just not enough room for the number of buttons required to make such a system work well. And many other traditional folk instruments (such as the bagpipes or the pipe & tabor) can only play in a very limited number of keys anyway.

Another regular event for the Woodside Morris Men was the combined local Morris Tours at which we danced with the Hammersmith Morris Men on the latter's home patch. This enabled between two and four sides to be fielded at the same time, as well as two or three men passing the hat around. But the thing I most remember about these Tours was once, while walking to the next dance spot, seeing one of the younger Hammersmith Men leap-frog over a red pillar-box! He was an Apprentice at Kew Gardens, I believe.

It was at the first or second of these combined Tours that I first met John Kirkpatrick, who was at that time playing a large, red "Shand" accordion, so named after the late popular Scottish Musician. Aged about nineteen at the time, John was already highly proficient on this instrument. A year or two later, his mother telephoned me to ask if I could recommend somewhere to get him an Anglo concertina for his 21st Birthday. Wheatstone & Co. being apparently defunct and Lachenal long out of business, I recommended *Harry Crabb and Son*, who made an excellent 40-key metal-ended C/G instrument specifically for him. John later became a well-known professional Folk musician, playing all the "free-reed" instruments and singing folk-songs of all eras (sometimes for Television), often in conjunction with his partner Sue Harris.

I also got to know Peter Boyce, a teacher from Chingford who ran at least one Morris team in the secondary school in which he taught. Some members of the Woodside Morris provided a few demonstrations of dancing for him at Chingford, so his pupils could see what the Morris was like with an adult side. This is how I met John Watcham, a fine player from whom I later bought an aged, but very serviceable, 31-key Jeffries Anglo. This was in the hope that my son Robert might wish to take up the Anglo. He did so, and later joined the Moulton Morris Men; he also occasionally plays for the Southampton-based Clausentium Morris, with which his son George has also danced in more recent times.

In 1970 it was all-change again and I got a new job in Newcastle-upon-Tyne, and took my leave of the Woodside Morris Men and the Circassian Circle Club. I duly joined the Newcastle Morris Men in the dual role of dancer and musician. The Newcastle Morris met once a week in a school hall in Jesmond, very similar to the one in Finchley, North London. We were joined occasionally by Tom Prince with his English concertina, and also seemed to collect visitors from the students at Newcastle University. An early one of these was Jim Catterall, but he went South to join the Thaxted Morris Men two or three years later. He was quite a competent melodion player from the start, but did not seem keen to dance.

Tom Prince – whom I had met previously at the ICA Competitions – was a very modest and unassuming man, with a great natural talent on the English Concertina; he also ran a group of "free reed" players in his home town of Consett. He could always be heard at his best when playing for the Rapper Dance – the speciality of Pit workers in Durham and the North-East. It was on those practice occasions when he turned up that I was able to put down my Jeffries and step in as the No. 2 in a Rapper side. Dave Varty generally danced No. 1 and Dave Bloomfield No.3. Bloomfield was totally at home with the dance, as his father had danced the Rapper from boyhood and he had learnt it from him as a youngster. He was thus able to perform the backward-somersault – one of the more spectacular ways of getting out of the "lock" where the five swords are held up briefly for all to see.

The Newcastle Morris Men went to Ring Meetings when they had the men and the means to do so, and I was with them at the 130th Meeting in Cambridge in July 1971 when the Sermon at the Sunday morning Service for the Morris Men was to be given by the Rev. Kenneth Loveless. I had not previously heard Ken in that to role although I had heard him sing and give a few talks in his unmistakable stentorian voice with its precise pronunciation. A Ring Meeting was one of those occasions which he relished, and he came thoroughly prepared for it – not least in his vestments, which included more than a little of the deep purple normally the prerogative of Bishops. His sermon made a great point of praising the activities of the Morris Men, and I remember particular phrases which came floating across the packed church such as "... these glo-o-o-rious Men ..." I must admit, though, to never having thought of myself as particularly glorious.

Another Ring Meeting which I particularly remember was the Staffordshire Meeting in September 1973, held at the Uttoxeter Racecourse. Over the next few years, however, the Newcastle Morris Men tended more to perform on their own patch and not to travel quite so regularly. As well as one-day local Tours (a "Day of Dance") there were traditional local events to attend, such as the "Baal-Fire," held in the village of Whalton (some ten miles north of where I live) on the 4th of July every year. This date was the original longest day of the year which had been determined in the early days of the Catholic Church. No-one realised at the time that the assumed length of the year was slightly in error, so that after a few hundred years there was an accumulated error of 13 days. Pope Gregory put it right by shifting the date to 13 days earlier in the Calendar and putting in place means for corrective annual adjustments. There were many riots following this ruling however, since a lot of people across Europe thought they had been unfairly deprived of the end of their lives – hence the call: "Give us back our 13 days!"

The occasion of the Baal Fire always was, and still is, marked by a large bonfire lit on the precise hour of 7:00pm. Whether it is a remnant of Pagan rituals which preceded the arrival of Christianity is not known, but nowadays it is a relaxed gathering of folk-performers, particularly players of the Northumbrian small-pipes, and any dancers or instrumentalists who care to come. Refreshments are available at the Beresford Arms in the centre of the village right next to the site of the bonfire.

For many years, during the first weekend after Easter, the Morpeth Gathering has also been held in the Town, which is about 25 miles North of Newcastle. Over the years the character of the meeting has varied; in the 1970s it was quite a free-and-easy occasion based on competitions for players of the Northumbrian small-pipes, along with classes for a few other instruments and performances. However, the time of year was not obviously chosen with outdoor performers in mind, since the weather has rarely been encouraging and it was quite possible to find snow on the streets. But we could dance at the Saturday Market and round and about the Town and pass the hat around without let or hindrance.

The occasion has lately much increased in size and gained in popularity, with a large Mayoral procession mid-morning on the Saturday and prize-giving and a Ceilidh in the evening – all given much prominence by *The Morpeth Herald* in the following week. After many years of not having a settled home, the Northumbrian Bagpipe Museum is now housed on the first floor of the medieval Morpeth Chantry in the centre of the Town, and The Northumbrian Bagpipe Society meets there regularly to play.

In those days, too, the Newcastle Morris men had an arrangement with The National Trust to visit a few of their local properties and dance for the public. One occasion that remains in my mind was at Wallington Hall, where we danced under the Clock-Tower in the early afternoon for quite a large crowd. While the dancers were doing their thing, I noticed my Managing Director; he had evidently spotted me in front of the dancers and was totally bemused at finding one of his Chief Engineers playing this strange instrument for a group of equally strange dancers. I still treasure the sight of the expression on his face.

Another regular date was the Summer Fete which was held on the Green by St. George's Church in Jesmond. We usually did two shows during the day, and I also played for a small group of children who performed part of a Maypole Dance. I made a recording of my music as an aide-memoir for the next year. As a concession to the ages of the children (about 8 or 9) I also inserted some slow music between the Figures so that they had plenty of time to sort themselves out; you can't afford mistakes in a Maypole Dance.

We met one unexpected school request, which was to give an indoor demonstration at the *Newcastle School for the Deaf*. The pupils were in this case aged about 11 to 13, and they seemed fascinated by it all. At the end they gathered round the dancers and the musician, looking at the costume and touching the buttons on the concertina. Any of them who wanted to attract my attention made a slight tap on the shoulder or arm. To what extent we succeeded in answering their questions I am not sure, but the whole experience was a rewarding one for one and all.

During the 1970s the fee for hiring a school hall had crept up and up, and gave us concerns as to how long we could continue in this way. While searching for alternatives, we approached Newcastle Racecourse to see what possibilities might lie there. They proved to be very helpful, and offered us the use of the Jockey's Accommodation, which was normally vacant between races. Prior to this, the overnight accommodation for Mini Ring Meetings had been provided by a church hall at Heddon-on-the-Wall, but it was far from satisfactory since the visiting Sides had to make the best of sleeping in the main hall and using the limited washing and toilet facilities which were available. When food was required, Dave Varty and his helpers were obliged to make the most of the very small kitchen.

The Jockey's Accommodation comprised a number of single-storey wooden huts, probably from a war or two back, which had been connected together to provide up to about 25 twin-bedded rooms (bring your own sleeping-bags) as well as showers and toilet facilities, a lounge, and quite a capable kitchen. Although it was all well past its 'sell-by date' it was what we needed for regular practices as well as for a Mini-Ring Meeting. The next ten years or so proved to be a Golden Age for the Club; Mini-Ring Meetings were held every year from 1982 until 1990, along with other regular engagements. For our own enjoyment we sometimes had a Day-of-Dance where the Newcastle Morris Men – plus a few friends such as the Durham Rams – did a day tour in a hired mini-coach but with no overnight stays or food provided.

In the year 1988 alone, we went to our regular local events, as above, and also attended the Thaxted Ring Meeting, the Barrow-in-Furness Ring Meeting (the Lake District) and ran our own Mini-Ring Meeting. Since in the Summer season we sometimes had several shows within weeks of each other I found it useful to make abbreviated Notes to leave in my concertina case as reminders of what we intended to perform. Some of these were just titles of the dances, and a few consisted of a few bars of the beginning of each tune, but that was all I needed.

In 1982 I made a C90 tape of most of the dance tunes that the Club were using at that time, and it had a small but enthusiastic circulation. And some two years later I made another tape, mainly to cover a Maypole Dance and the Ascot-under-Wychwood tradition, but that Tape had a smaller circulation. Two or three years after this I happened to encounter a local Scout Leader in Morris kit who had obviously got one of my first tapes and was anxious to demonstrate his progress. I listened and the music was really not at all bad but one thing filled me with dismay: he was holding the instrument upside down! I had not the heart to tell him so – which I now feel I should have done at the risk of consigning all his work to the scrapheap – so I made some non-committal remarks and left as best I could.

During one of our earlier Day-of-Dance meetings Kenneth Loveless had joined us and came fully kitted out as a Morris Man. He evidently was having trouble with his knees and hadn't come with one of his concertinas either, so mostly he just watched the dancers with interest and applauded where appropriate but didn't do much else. I remember him appearing behind me after a Headington dance by the Newcastle Men and, whilst puffing on his pipe, muttering "nice Riggs Phil", which I classed as praise indeed at the time.

And then, in March 1987, the Morris Ring asked the Newcastle Morris Men to host a Representatives' Meeting in the Newcastle area, and it was known that Kenneth Loveless intended to be present. It was however considered that, as he was now getting on in years, he merited more comfort and privacy than the Jockey' Quarters could offer. I lived not too far away and had a spare bedroom; I could also boast a nodding acquaintance with Kenneth and, moreover, I was a fellow Anglo concertina player. I was duly volunteered and on the Friday evening of the Meeting weekend I collected him from the racecourse and took him back home for the night. Although they had previously observed him from a distance, my family had not come across anything quite like Kenneth before. However, they had no chance to savour the experience just then, for we had to set off early on the Saturday to embark on the business of the day. This was then rounded off by a meal (prepared by the Newcastle men) and followed in the evening by much dancing, singing and reminiscing. A special feature was the invited presence of one of the old Royal Earsdon Sword Dancers, and he and Ken together made the evening quite a memorable one.

Kenneth was obviously in his element, and showed no signs of flagging nor the slightest inclination of returning to his bed; I, for my part, resolved to stick it out as long as required. Eventually when two o'clock in the morning had passed, numbers of Morris Men began to run out of steam and, one by one, they disappeared to their cubicles. I eventually ran the Earsdon man home and arrived with Ken at my house a little after three-thirty am. My wife was not expecting such a late session although she did not pass much comment at the time. We did, however, hear odd chinking noises from Kenneth's room until well after four o'clock. Not all that much later that same morning breakfast turned out to be a long and leisurely affair, although Ken himself ate virtually nothing but drank innumerable cups of freshly ground coffee. He was absolutely charming; he talked to the family and listened attentively to my daughter playing her flute and made encouraging remarks. On request, he did show us his concertina although neither of us played. In fact, we had never seemed to discuss concertinas at all over many years.

When all the coffee had gone and it was time to leave he was most gracious in his thanks to my wife for having him to stay. She particularly recalls how he commented favourably on the state of cleanliness of our lavatory. We were slightly surprised at this, but then I remembered the Jockeys' Quarters and reflected that he may well have stayed in some pretty odd places in his time – especially during his Naval career. The Royal Navy always insisted that 'The Heads' should be in pristine condition at all times!

After he was gone my wife Jennifer commented casually on the strange, sweet, and very persistent scent left in the room which Ken had recently occupied and wondered what sort of aftershave he had used, to be followed almost immediately by the realisation that this was not a cosmetic that he would need. She was not acquainted with the ways of a High Church Anglican so I explained that (being Lent) it had been necessary for him to compress his various Religious Offices into the space between returning home and breakfast; and the perfume was undoubtedly that of incense, not aftershave.

A few days later we received through the post a short but most courteous letter of thanks from Kenneth for our hospitality at the weekend. I remember particularly the manner of the date, written with the day in Arabic and the month in Roman numerals. The script itself was written with a broad-nib and was so bold that only a few words seemed to fill the whole page. Like the man, the hand was definitely larger than life, and quite unique.

In 1988 an English Concertina player named Steve Desmond, who had recently relocated north to take up a position at the *Durham College of Agriculture & Horticulture*, began advertising for people to join his proposed *North Eastern Concertina Players* (NECP). I got in touch and in no time at all I found myself in the job of Secretary and arranged for some of the meetings to take place in a small room at Newcastle Racecourse. People attended from a wide catchment area covering up to Edinburgh, Carlisle and Yorkshire.

Steve himself was particularly proud of owning a Baritone English instrument as well as a standard Treble. Most of those who joined were also English players and generally could read music, if a little slowly. Several of the most enthusiastic players, however, were Anglo people and could play by ear but couldn't manage too well when it came to reading music; we were also never sure of who was going to turn up on any given day. But there was some effort over time to produce collections of music to fit the needs of all the various players and their different abilities, and it certainly helped.

But then, in 1990, our world showed signs of falling apart. The Racecourse put plans in hand to demolish the group of ancient huts we used and replace them with much better and more permanent accommodation for the jockeys. For the time-being we were, however given alternative space in some of the other buildings on the site, and went on to hold a very successful local Day of Dance in July 1991.

In February 1992 Mike Noone – a founder member of the Newcastle Morris Men – sadly died after a short illness. This was quite a blow to the Team, and there was a period when practices had to be cancelled due to poor attendance. We did, however, manage to support our regular commitments in following years. Then in 1993 Steve Desmond, who had started the NECP, had a change of job and was also due to leave the Northeast permanently at the end of the Academic Year. The last "local" meeting of the NECP was held later in the year 1992 at Nunnery House, a small hotel in Cumbria.

Following my own retirement in 1995, I bought an electric piano and spent some years revisiting baroque and jazz music, and generally wound down on the Anglo – but it never actually went away! Then, in 2019, some members of my family, together with one or two dancers from the Newcastle Morris Men, all suggested I should set about recording a few of the tunes I had played on the Anglo Concertina over the years. I thought this was a good idea, but did not want to restrict the choice only to Morris Tunes, and included some sea shanties, Northumbrian music, Playford music and madrigals, amongst other oddments, to add to what I had already recorded.

Every now and again, those of us in the NMM (who are still able) meet up for a glass of beer or a cup of coffee. If we touch on old times, the phrase which always seems to crop up is: "They were great times, weren't they?" They were indeed.

Phil Ham
April 2022

GARY COOVER

A longtime fan of the concertina ever since discovering British traditional music while in college, Gary was inspired to learn to play the Anglo concertina through the music of John Kirkpatrick and John Watcham.

In 2013 he published his first Anglo instruction book, *Anglo Concertina in the Harmonic Style*, which included tunes from William Kimber, John Kirkpatrick, Jody Kruskal, Bertram Levy, Kenneth Loveless, Brian Peters, and Andy Turner.

The success of this book led to the creation of Rollston Press, which today has nearly 30 titles in its catalog, half of which are instruction books for a wide variety of music especially arranged for the Anglo concertina.

All of Gary's books utilize a simple and popular "play-by-number" tablature system based on 19th century Anglo tutors. Most of the books feature video instruction – Rollston Press was one of the first music publishers to incorporate QR code links that provide video and audio links to YouTube videos and SoundCloud audio recordings.

FOR MORE INFORMATION ABOUT THE ANGLO CONCERTINA:

The Anglo-German Concertina: A Social History Volume 1 & 2 by Dan Worrall

www.concertina.com

www.concertina.net

CONCERTINA BOOKS FROM ROLLSTON PRESS

Anglo Concertina in the Harmonic Style

Easy Anglo 1-2-3

Christmas Concertina

Civil War Concertina

75 Irish Session Tunes for Anglo Concertina

Pirate Songs for Concertina

Sailor Songs for Concertina

Sea Songs for 20-Button Anglo Concertina

Cowboy Concertina

A Garden of Dainty Delights

The Jeffries Duet Concertina Tutor

The Anglo Concertina Music of John Watcham

The Anglo Concertina Music of John Kirkpatrick

Anglo Concertina from Beginner to Master

AVAILABLE FROM AMAZON.COM,
RED COW MUSIC, AND OTHER FINE RETAILERS

Printed in Great Britain
by Amazon

47970546R00066